Power of the V

Contact Us:

Ki-Stone Books, Inc.
P.O. Box 78761
Los Angeles, CA 90016

Book Inquiries:

1-866-965-2224

To order additional copies of this book:

www.kistonebooks.com
or
1-800-266-5564

Printed in the United States of America
9 8 7 6 5 4 3 2 1 0

53217

Contents

DEDICATION

I dedicate this book to all of the girls and women in the world who have yet to recognize the power that is in their possession.

Being a female is truly a gift from God. Every woman should know her esteemed position on earth, as well as their worth that is within. This personal dedication is an acknowledgment to all women who aspire to be the best in whatever they set out to become and accomplish in life, personally and professionally.

Let this book offer you the strength to never give up, and a foundation to stand on.

PURPOSE

We all were put here on earth for a purpose. I believe my purpose on earth is to educate women all over the world about the power that they hold within. If I can change the life of one girl or woman I have accomplished my purpose.

I have come to recognize the gift that God has bestowed upon me, and I have chosen to use that gift to spread the word of wisdom of the "Power of the V."

Purpose is given to all; purpose is to acknowledge what real purpose represents and purpose is to be shared. With this book I have shared my purpose.

"When you find your purpose, you find yourself."

Woman is more fitted than man to make exploration and take colder action in nonviolence . . . there is no occasion or women to consider themselves subordinate or inferior to men . . . Woman is the companion of man, gifted with equal mental capacity . . . if by strength is meant moral power, and then woman is immeasurably man's superior. If nonviolence is the law of our being, the future is with women . . .

—Mahatma Gandhi

POWER OF THE V

The power of the V has been a treasure for women since the beginning of time. It has been the downfall for many leaders and officials, and a tool for many women who have used their V to achieve job promotions, men, marriage, money etc . . .

When you think of the V, think of passion, profit, power, and pleasure.

ACKNOWLEDGMENT

I would like to take this moment to acknowledge my daughters; Dominece, Tameika, Jonice, and Sidnee Watts, and my mother, Margie Watts. The five of you helped shape my life over the past twenty-five years, and it was in my absence that I took notice of the blessings that God has bestowed upon me.

I acknowledge all of your strength and courage, and the ability to make decent choices under extreme circumstances, which has shaped you into the beautiful souls you are today. My acknowledgment is a form of recognition of what you ladies truly mean to me.

A SPECIAL THANK YOU

I would like to start off by thanking my daughter, Dominece Watts, for assisting me in the early stages of my book project.

A special thank you goes out to my friend and Chief Editor, Gayle Chambers-Smith for making this project number one in her life for an entire year. A special thank you also is extended to, Ingrid Hutt, Heather Hutt, Lesley Hall, Linda Morgan, Marie-Francoise Theodore, Claudio Sgaravizz, Phyllis Lewis, Christina Shack, Monica Fuselier, Nikia T. Smith, Victoria Walker, Autumn McCoy, Brenda Webb and Joseph Marich, Jr.

I also want to thank everyone that took the time to read and critique the first chapter, and voice their comments and opinions. Last but not least, I would like to express my gratitude to each and every one of my investors that trusted, and believed in this project and for believing in me.

POSITIVE & POWERFUL WOMEN

Let's take a look at some of your positive & powerful women of today and yesterday.

Positive or powerful woman raised a lot of our influential men. Take our 44th President of the United States of America, Barack Obama. He was raised by his single mother and grandmother. Here are just a few in a long list of positive and powerful women who have influenced men and woman over the years. Oprah Winfrey, a global role model, actress, entrepreneur and one of the most powerful women in television today. Former Secretary of State Condoleezza Rice was one of the most powerful women in her position when she was in office. Hilary Clinton, our new Secretary of State continues to be a positive leader among women. Actress/Ambassador, Angelina Jolie; CEO Debra Lee of BET; Motivational Speaker, Suze Orman; Chairman and CEO, Indra Nooyi; Women Advocate, Zanib Salbi; Congresswoman, Maxine Waters; First Lady of California, Maria Shriver; Television Judge, Glenda Hatchet; President & CEO of Johnson & Johnson, Linda Johnson-Rice; San Francisco District Attorney, Kamala Harris; Gospel Singer, Cee Cee Winans; Chile's President, Michelle Bachelet; Breast Cancer Awareness Ambassador, Nancy Brinker; Founder of U.S. National Teaching Corps, Wendy Kopp; President of Ariel Investment, Mellody Hubson;

Here are some of our new and upcoming positive, powerful, and influential women: Model/Producer/Actress and Talk Show Host Tyra Banks; Talk Show Host, Ellen DeGeneres; Singer and Actress, Vanessa Williams; Actress, Queen Latifah; Actress, Jada-Pinket-Smith; Hip Hop Queen, Mary J. Blige; R&B Singer and Actress, Alicia Keys; Actress, Angela Bassett; Business Woman, Madeeha Hasan Odhaib; Golfer, Lorena Ochoa; Gospel Singers, Mary Mary and Yolanda Adams; Tennis Stars, Serena and Venus Williams; R&B Singer and Actress, Beyonce; R&B Singer, Mariah Carey; R&B singer, Keyshia Cole; and let's not forget our first African American First Lady, Michelle Obama, the power force and confident woman behind President Barack Obama. There are also the power women who we've lost: Mother Theresa, Princess Diana, and Civil Rights Pioneer, Dorothy Irene Height.

Special acknowledgment goes out to all the positive and powerful females, school teachers, doctors, nurses, lawyers, entrepreneurs, servicewomen and single mothers.

These are women that have set the bar high enough to reach their goals through drive and determination. These are the women that people look up to. These are the women that refuse to exploit themselves.

I have nothing but total respect for a positive and powerful woman, such as my mother, Margie Watts. She is also a positive and powerful woman with moral standards who carries respect as her shield. She never indulged in tobacco, alcohol or drugs. She remained positive, even in a non-positive environment while raising eight children in a two bedroom, run-down, roach-infested apartment in South Central, Los Angeles. She lived on a welfare check and food stamps while my father decided to take a permanent leave-of-absence from the work force. Her positive attitude and strength, which she inherited from her mother, played a powerful role in my life. She displayed all of the positive qualities I continue to strive for today.

I hold in high regard every positive and powerful woman, and I respect those who respect themselves. I salute women who stand up for what's right and who refuse to compromise. I congratulate women who have a higher education. I applaud all single mothers who struggle to raise a child or children on their own, yet never stop trying to be the best mother they can be.

In my lifetime, I have heard many men say, "It's hard to find a good woman in America." As an American man, I would like to disagree with those men, but I find it hard to do so at times. As I studied the different cultures of women, I found there are still some women in America who believe that the man should be the leader in the relationship, and the woman should be a follower. I have also discovered that many women have traded places with men. There are more and more women becoming CEO's, CFO's and Presidents of Corporations, earning their own money, and in some cases, earning more than men.

I believe there are good women right here in America.

The bible says, "He *who* finds a wife finds a good *thing*, and obtains favor from the Lord." **Proverbs 18.22**

Attention ladies! Stop looking for your husband, and let your husband *find you.*

INTRODUCTION

The V is remarkable and incredible. It's the only thing that can outlast and outperform the penis 1,000 to 1. The V also has the ability to achieve orgasm from three different sources starting with the vaginal walls, the clitoris, and the "g-spot," whereas the penis only has one.

Could you imagine a canal the size of an Almond opening up to the size of a Watermelon and returning to its original size without losing an inch? There is nothing else on this planet that can duplicate a similar feat.

Women across the world believe it's the V that holds the power. From the beginning of time there has been only one thing that brings joy, pain and life, all at the same time.

Chapter One

Power of the V

June 15, 2008

Dear Dominece and Tameika,

I pray that the two of you and your children are doing well by the time this letter reaches your hands. As for myself, I'm doing ok considering my circumstances. It pains me that I've been absent from your lives because of my poor choice to over-bill Medicare and file false tax returns, leading me to federal prison for the past nine years.

To you, Dominece, I would like to express how sorry I am for not being there to protect you from becoming a victim of abuse during your first semester in high school. Although this tragic event occurred over eight years ago when you were only 14, I'm sure you continue to have difficulties dealing with the pain and ramifications of that tragedy, as well as the nights you spent in the hospital unable to breathe, not knowing where your next breath would come from because you suffered multiple asthma attacks.

To you Tameika, I deeply apologize for not being a part of your early years. For many years, I was under the impression that your mother had an abortion, which I supported when I found out she was pregnant, but since then I've come to realize that you are a gift from God, and I welcome you into my life. You should also know that today I believe in Pro-Life; however, I understand if a woman has an abortion due to serious health issues, critical birth defects, rape or if the mother has an addiction that can be passed on to the baby. You make life worth living and I love you more than you could ever imagine, and I want you to know that.

It wasn't until today, after receiving my Father's Day cards from both of you that I realized I should have told the two of you many years ago, long before you girls became mothers, that all women are special, talented and have many attributes that are exclusive only to women. It appears that a lot of women these days are surrendering their precious gifts to men, leaving themselves powerless, including you and your sister. Between the two of you there are five children and four baby daddies. None of them have a job, a car, a place of their own, or good credit, not to mention they all have criminal records.

I have also come to realize that I'm no different than anyone else. I have made mistakes, and my life's journey is no more than a story of the human condition, and about how faith and determination brought me through difficult times. Your dad's life experiences will show you how an individual can uplift himself from circumstances of wrong doing even though I believed it was for all the right reasons. My failure and success does not define who I am, but they have shaped who I have become. While others used prison to serve time, I used it to teach myself how to properly read and write.

You and your sister work ten hour shifts just to keep a roof over your head and food on the table. When you girls get home from work you rush to prepare dinner, spend hours cleaning the house, washing dishes, and getting clothes ready for the next day. When you finally get to bed you have some man trying to climb on top of you because he's well rested, full, and horny from sitting around the house all day playing X-box. A woman was not meant to carry that type of burden on her shoulders alone.

I believe you girls are worth more than that, but you too need to believe that as well. Break the "Emotional Dysfunctional Roller Coaster." Know the power that has been given to you that places YOU in control, and not the man.

Our Father in Heaven said that He would never leave us or forsake us in time of trouble and as your father here on earth, I will never leave you or forsake you in your time of need. The past can't be undone, but our future can be formed from this day forward. As young women, you deserve the best from your father, as well as any other man that comes into your life. Again, forgive me for missing birthdays, graduations, proms and the birth of your children, my grandchildren. Not only was I, your father absent; I was absent from our entire family.

Regardless of your choices whether they be good or bad, I am proud of your accomplishments, and the women you girls have become. The love I have for each one of you will never change.

To you Dominece, the next time you find yourself going through something with a man, or your relationship; I hope to be there to offer you support and guidance. And remember, my door is open to you and your sisters 24/7.

Love
Your Dad

THIRTY-TWO DAYS LATER

After serving nine long years in federal prison, I was released on the morning of July 21, 2008. I arrived at my mother's home that evening where friends and family were there to welcome me home. My mother prepared a home-cooked meal especially for me. Later that night, I lay there in the tub with my eyes closed giving thanks to God for bringing me through this past journey and all that I endured. I settled in, and got comfortable on the sofa where I immediately fell asleep somewhere around midnight. I had no idea how exhausted was. I suppose the anxiety of being released the night before, being unable to sleep, and that long uncomfortable bus ride took a toll on my body.

At three o'clock in the morning, the telephone rang. It was my 22-year-old daughter, Dominece.

"Hello!" I said, as I struggle to find my voice.

"Dad, I needed to talk to someone. I don't have anyone else to talk to. I know you just got home, but I need to talk."

"What's wrong, baby, do you need for me to come where you are?

"I'm on my way to you, Dad. Bye." She hung up the telephone.

I rolled off the couch, got myself together, and waited for my daughter to arrive. Approximately twenty minutes later, she pulls in front of my mother's house. I hear a car door slam so I turned on the porch light and looked out of the window. I see my daughter running up to the front door carrying her sons, one in each arm. She's yelling "DAD! HEY, DAD! IT'S DOMINECE. OPEN THE DOOR!" I opened the door; both of her boys are crying and irritated, because she had awakened them from their sleep. I took one of the boys from her and went to the closet to get a pillow and a blanket. I laid them down on the couch, and they both went back to sleep as soon as their heads hit the pillow. I then said, "Dominece, calm down. I need you to stop crying."

Dominece finally regained her composure.

I lowered my voice and said, "Have you lost your mind, yelling out my name like a crazy woman? The last thing that your grandmother needs is for one of her nosey neighbors to wake up and call the police. Why do you have these kids out here at three o'clock in the morning, anyway?" The two of us headed to the kitchen and I made tea for both of us. We sat at the kitchen table across from one another. She kicked off her house slippers, threw her purse across the room, and slammed her car keys on the dinette table, nearly breaking the glass on the table.

"I'm sorry to bother you but I couldn't sleep, Dad. My boyfriend AJ and I had a fight.

"Did he hit you? Are you hurt? Where is he?"

"No, he didn't hit me, but he did hurt me when he walked out on me in the middle of the night. I don't know what I am going to do. I have no idea when he is even coming back. What did I do to make him so angry? I'm clueless, Dad. I tried everything to be a good woman to AJ. I cook, clean the house, look after the kids, pay the bills, work and I do my best to be a good woman. I have never cheated on him. I'm there for him regardless of what it is. When it comes to sex, he gets it when he wants it, and how he wants it."

"That's one of your problems; stop dropping it like its hot and picking it up like its cold. Where is the value in all this? What do you get out of this relationship?"

"What should I do, Dad?"

"Let me tell you about the birds and the V's."

"I am twenty-two years old, Dad, and have two kids. I do not need to know about the birds, and the bees. I learned that a long time ago. Besides, I came over here for advice regarding my relationship," said Dominece.

"I'm not talking about the birds and the bees. I'm talking about the birds and the V's. I am talking about the value of your worth, your power. I'm trying to tell you that YOU HOLD THE POWER!"

"Dad, lower your voice before you wake Grandma and the kids

"I'm sorry I get emotional when I think that someone is trying to take advantage of my daughters. I know I can be over-protective at times."

"You said that I have power. What kind of power do I have?"

I went on to explain my thoughts about the power of the V.

Here is what I believe:

All women have the power of the V, the power of the vagina. It's the true power of every woman along with her integrity, morality, respect, loyalty, confidence, and her wisdom. Dominece, like many women, has given a man too much power over her. Every woman today needs to realize the power of the V and treat their bodies, minds, and souls like the precious gifts they are. Many years ago, when I was growing up, I watched men work while their wives stayed home, raised the kids, and took care of the household.

I explained to my daughter that it is young women like her, and the others like her who do not know the power they have. Because they are not aware of their own power, they give up their power to the men in their lives. If women band together and go on a vagina strike for one year, women could rule the world. In the Greek play by Aristophanes called *Lysistrata*, the title character calls on all women of Greece to refrain from having sex with their husbands until a peace treaty is signed to end the Peloponnesian War. Her plan works and the war ends. That is the power of the V.

One of the first things a woman should do before she decides to give up her virginity is evaluate her power and her self-worth. Own that power. Use that power to think before acting. Women are priceless. The V-is PRICELESS.

My daughter then asked me, "Why do you feel I'm priceless Dad?"

I went on to explain my thoughts.

Women have the power and the ability to carry life inside them for nine months. When they are not pregnant, they are reminded of this miraculous life-giving ability once a month. It is this ability to hold and give life that should give women a solid understanding of their own power.

Women hold the true power because they have what men need, want, and desire. The day women realize that they hold the power, and not the man they think they're so in love with, is the day their lives will change forever. It is a fact that European women understand their power and worth. It is taught to them at a young age.

I finally told my daughter that she needs to stop crying and get control of her emotions. I told her to go home, relax, and stand in front of the mirror and take a real good look at herself and think about what I was telling her. There is nothing a woman cannot do when she puts her mind to it. A man's power is limited and hers is not. I am not saying that men do not have power.

Men often times strip women of their self-confidence to make themselves feel more powerful and to make the woman more dependent on them, making her feel she cannot leave. A good healthy relationship is based on mutual respect and an equal balance of power, in other words a man should enrich and enhance the life of his woman and not take from it.

Both men and women use sex as a power play. Sex—or withholding—sex should not be used as a form of punishment or reward. If a woman decides to stop having sex with her partner, for whatever reason, he will probably see this as her sending a message to him that says she doesn't care or love him. He may feel that way because she didn't allow him to control the situation. Now if the couple is not married, denying him sex is the woman's choice. No one can, or should force a woman to have sex if she doesn't want to - Period.

If the woman withholds sex from him he may become very angry; his entire personality may change right in front of her eyes. She will see the change, but she should not let this keep her from her goal—empowerment. This is the beginning of tapping into the power women hold from within.

After explaining this, I said, "And don't be surprised if he tries to force himself on you."

"Force himself on me?" my daughter asked.

"Yes."

"Why would he try to do that?"

"Because you said no, but if he ever does it, the first thing you do is leave; the second thing you do is call your father. For a man to force himself on a woman is low and you don't need to be in that type of relationship."

I went on to explain to her that her man may act as if he's waiting, thinking you'll change your mind and put out, but he will most certainly be looking to get him some from somewhere else. Most young men don't sit around and wait for one woman to give it up.

Men tell women that they love them and that they are the only woman for him, but unless the woman has a ring on her finger, that man is going to find ways of taking advantage of her every chance he gets. Unfortunately, sometimes he will take advantage even if they *are* married.

My daughter simply couldn't understand this. She felt that if he said he loves her, she should do whatever he says he needs her to do. I continued to explain that when a man is in love with a woman—especially if she has children—he should not by laying around all day playing video games or hanging out with his friends. He should be working or looking for a job to help take care of those kids, regardless if they are his or not. *That* is what *real* men do.

"AJ is a good man Dad," Dominece says to me, at this point.

"Most women try to make something out of nothing. Again, if he doesn't show you the basic respect needed in a healthy relationship like having a job, owning a car, or being willing to help pay bills, and have his own place to lay his head, he is not the right one for you, baby. You can spend five, ten, even fifteen years waiting for him to make a change that may never come. Change has to be in him for him to take that next step. I hate to say this, but it leaves me no choice. AJ is a loser."

"To say that AJ is a loser may be a bit much, Dad. I know him. Do you think he would wait if I hold back?" she asked me.

"Boys usually wait a few days, young men may wait for a few weeks and older men will probably wait for a few months if he sees a future in that woman. Boys and young men find it hard to adapt to sudden changes that young women make in a sexual relationship."

She agreed to give some serious thought to what I was saying and agreed to try to put into practice some of the thoughts I had been discussing with her.

I also told her that I think women should not be trying to think like men, but rather, men should start trying to think like women. It is women who need to be understood. Women are the more complicated ones. In fact, if more men took the time and thought like a woman they would have a better idea how to treat a real woman, and their relationships would have more substance.

"But before you leave, I have a question to ask you. Do you love AJ?"

"Yes," she says.

"At what level?"

"What do you mean 'what level'?"

"Did you know there were seven levels to love?"

"No, I thought love was love."

"Let me explain. Have a seat," I say and I smile. I'm going to tell my daughter how to begin her journey to discover her own Power of the V.

After describing the seven levels of love (*see Chapter 2*), I asked Dominece again what level of love she thinks she is in with AJ.

"I would say that AJ and I are in level three," she tells me.

"Three isn't bad for a young couple." I reply.

"I guess. I really thought I was at a higher level with AJ, but I guess I'm not. OK, let me get the boys and go home." said Dominece.

"Leave them here. Pick them up later in the morning. Let grandpa have some play time with his grandkids." I tell Dominece. She smiles.

"I'll pick them up later and thank you, Dad. I love you."

"I love you, too, and the next time you get ready to start a new relationship with a man be sure to say these words to him . . .

If you want me,

You got me."

"If you get me,

You keep me."

"If you lose me,

You lost me."

"I like that Dad; I'll remember that."

"And one more thing; don't complain about it, if you're not going to do anything about it."

"And I hold the power, right?" Dominece asked before leaving.

"You hold the power, but remember there are two relationships going on simultaneously. There's the one in the bedroom and the one outside the bedroom. The most important part of any relationship between a man and a woman is the one spent outside of the bedroom."

I stood up and walked Dominece to the front door; I hugged and kissed my baby. Then I whispered in her ear, "Never underestimate your power. Remember that, baby. The V has the power to rule the world."

"I got it."

"Good! I'm going back to bed. Goodnight," I said to her as I yawned.

"Hey, Dad, do you believe that a man could make love to a woman's mind?"

"Absolutely. Make love to the mind first, the heart and body will follow." I answered.

Dominece turned around, looks at me and says.

"I'm glad you're home Dad."

"I gave them nine years, the rest belong to you, your sisters, my grandkids and myself; now you drive safe going home."

"I will."

I watched her drive away. After closing the door, I turned off the lights and went back to sleep, happy that I could help.

I am quite sure that many of you think I was wrong to sit down and talk to my daughter about her power, but if not me, then who? As a parent should I release my daughter into the streets to learn the wrong thing from someone that doesn't give a damn about her, or what path her life takes? Should I allow her to make the same mistakes that many of us have made? Should the responsibility of raising my children be the school systems or mine?

I believe that if more fathers take the time to talk with their daughters, and show them an example of how men should treat them, our young girls will grow up to learn to respect themselves. And the rate of teen pregnancy would drop. Being a father means more than providing finances or what we buy them from the mall or other shopping outlets. It's about teaching our girls how to respect themselves, and how to become ladies.

Womanhood starts at the age of 18 and in some countries earlier but; becoming a "Lady" is something that is taught by example. As a father you never want to see your daughters go through unnecessary drama. To see my daughters grow from little girls to adults, to having their own children, makes me proud. All I can hope for now is that Dominece takes what I shared with her and uses it to become a woman of strength.

Chapter Two

The Seven Levels of Love

ZERO LEVEL OF LOVE

Love is desired by all.

There is no love in this level, which makes it self-explanatory. This level of love offers nothing, not even a strong friendship.

I believe that every man and woman should experience true love at least once. A person who is unable to reach at least a 'level one love' in my book, is someone who is totally self-centered, or who has been so emotionally damaged by something in their past that it is impossible for them to find and experience love. This person is often selfish, stingy, has a negative attitude, not to mention they are usually mean and heartless. This level can also cause you to become a 'HATER.' This is simply a case of not knowing how to love you and true love starts with loving yourself. How can you love someone without loving yourself?

For women only: Would you really want to have someone in your life that pretends to love you but really doesn't? Of course not, in fact, a person that has no love for self can only pretend to have love for someone else.

FIRST LEVEL OF LOVE

Love is desired by all.

"I love your hair"

"I love your shoes"

"I love your car"

"I love your make-up"

"I love your pictures"

"I love your new cell phone"

"I love your earrings"

"I love your cooking"

The first level of love is what I call "Basic Love." This is when a woman shows a little affection for the man while dating for the first six-months. It also bridges the gap between a friendship and a relationship. This is not to say that friends can't hang out for months at a time, but we all know it's rarely done today. When two people are spending a lot of time together an attraction is there. In most cases, by the time the sixth month arrives sex usually has already made its way into the bedroom.

Today, we use the word "love" to describe things from hair to food.

Using the word *love* to describe casual things diminishes the word especially when it is used to express emotional feelings for another person.

When the word *love* is taken out of casual conversations and only used in the context of a relationship, the impact of the word means so much more.

Where other levels of love offer a much more fulfilling type of love, level one allows you to get to know the other person without any long-term attachment. In the event the two of you decide to end the relationship the break-up will not hurt as much. No level of love should be taken for granted, and should be looked upon as a way to share your inner beauty with another human being. So, the next time you tell someone that you love them, research the true meaning of the word love and what it is supposed to represent. Most women or girls might think sex is an expression of love. The truth is, in some cases, especially in the early stages of a relationship, sex is only sex; there is no real passion. You should never confuse sex with love.

It is a good time to do an anger level check at this level of love. It is important to know if you're dealing with a level-headed person, or a Looney Tune. I'm not saying that you should intentionally make your man angry with you. What I am saying is, before a level two relationship is established you should already have had a disagreement or a slight argument. You should be aware of how he reacts when he becomes angry. When he is angry does he display signs of violence, does he cuss at you when expressing his anger? Does he take his anger out on you when he is really angry with someone else? Does he shut down, or does he control the situation in a calm manner without having an emotional attitude toward you? These are critical questions you need to ask yourself and discover the answers before becoming involved with any man.

Remember! This is the first level, and you are finding out whether or not you can share your life with the person you're involved with.

SECOND LEVEL OF LOVE

Love is desired by all

A level two love includes level one love, but with stronger affection for one another. You begin to enjoy one another's company much more, you show signs of affection, when you are not with each other you think about him or her, and also the level of communication between you two increases. During this level you may find yourself calling the person you are beginning to love several times a day. I call it, "Checking In." It also causes you to want to know each other's friends and family. At this level you find yourself wanting to be closer, like spending nights at one another's home, and eating off of the same plate when you go out to dinner.

Some might possibly mistake this level to be a level three or being "in love" (I will explain why being in love with someone doesn't really exist later). To love at this level only gets better with time. Once two people reach this stage of love, one would have already exposed himself emotionally. Either he's a good man, a decent man, a bad man or a psycho.

At this level if you're not careful, a man can use this level of love to his advantage. His intention may be to use or abuse you while he is engaged in this relationship. I'm not saying it's not okay to reach this level, however, one should not become so blind from love that it consumes your thoughts and kills your common sense, causing you to live in fantasy land and allow yourself to be treated badly.

Remember! Love is an expression of how a person feels about you. It doesn't mean he's a God.

If you ever feel uncertain about how you are feeling. Re-visit level one and remind yourself how you got to level two. It's a reminder of your true feelings.

True Love is not supposed to hurt.

THIRD LEVEL OF LOVE

Love is desired by all

Level three love includes level one and two, but with an added twist.

Level three love should include readiness and the desire to solve conflicts. At this level, a solid friendship should already be established. Friendship is the foundation of any type of relationship. At this level of love, a woman can become insincere in her relationship if she doesn't have the primary building-block for a healthy relationship, which is "Trust." Trust is a factor that must be a part of any level of love, without trust you have nothing.

In this level a woman who is not cautious can experience a lot of hurt and pain if she is not careful. Nothing hurts more than this level of love relationship, because so much must be put into it. It also can be thought of as a tool that brings two people closer. In fact, this level can bring you one step closer to wedding bells. By this stage, an average person will be calling their partner at least four or five times a day. The two of you probably have keys to one another's home or apartment. You are probably drinking out of the each other's glass, or cup without realizing it; this has become an everyday normal thing.

At this level of love a couple may begin to shower together without being embarrassed. Your partner might place a blanket on you while you are asleep and kiss you on the forehead. You smile during your sleep because you think it's sweet.

Most women who are at this level are having conversations with their partner about marriage. How long does it take to move from a level one to a level three love? This is what most of you may be asking yourselves. It's simple; in order to develop a level one love into a level three love just listen to your partner. Start sharing up to 50 percent of your available time with your man, including doing things outside of your home. You should notice an increase in the number of times compliments are given. Continuously learn and grow with one another. Be in touch with his feelings as he is in tune with yours. Pursue new and different experiences, and lastly, give without expectations. And let's not forget sacrifice for the betterment of the relationship. Your soul should thirst for real love.

This is where trust begins to strengthen.

FOURTH LEVEL OF LOVE

Love is desired by all

A level four love, just as the other levels, is additive. In a level four love you begin to spend quality time with one another. There are more serious thoughts of becoming one. You often feel as though you never want to be separated from that person for long periods of time. This is when you swear there are dozens of humming birds flying around in your stomach, and no, I did not make a mistake when I said humming birds. I believe the feelings of butterflies are for teenagers.

At this level you both know one another's personality, and a support system has pretty much been established between the two of you. A love relationship is priority along with other important things such as going to work, paying bills, etc. The refinement of love has already been established, and there are no misleading thoughts or concerns. Once again, as I stated in level three, give without any expectations, and give without being asked.

Being at level four love is not about how fast you can make love, it's about how long you can make love last. The secret to keeping this level of love on a solid foundation is to tell the one you love that you love them often. And mean it sincerely. Both of you should find romantic things to do together like getting up with the sunrise and don't leave out the small things like taking long walks together. Sign up for dance classes, cooking classes, wine tasting or a massage class. If your partner does not agree to do some of the things you suggest, this is in no way an indication that he loves you any less. It only means he's not interested, just like you may not be interested in some of the things that he chooses. Again, complement one another frequently, and always consider everyday as a special day.

This level of love might remind you of your teenage years when you first thought you were in love. Notes are passed in the classroom; kisses are blown across the room when eye contact is made. You are no longer afraid to publicly display your affection with your partner. Believe it or not some older people will look at you and think it is sweet, whereas some single people will watch and wish they were in your shoes. I have another name for this level; I call it "Hot Butter Love." This level will make you leave a trail of clothes from the front door to the bedroom. Romance and Passion will become your best friends.

Love is no longer complicated and love is no longer ordinary. Your relationship starts to feel like one beautiful paradise. The best is being brought out of one another and your partner becomes your quiet storm.

FIFTH LEVEL OF LOVE

Love is desired by all

This level of love is a tricky one. It's the level of love that can have you believing that your partner is perfect and he can do no wrong. You find yourself committed, and I mean *deeply* committed. I call this level of love, "**Special Love**."

Of course sex and love-making become part of the ordinary along with other things like, paying bills, planning vacations together, and making retirement plans with one another. At this level the two of you should already be married and crazy about one another. You're able to read one another and when your partner is hurting, you hurt. In this level of love there is usually a strong spiritual connection. You automatically do things for one another without any hesitation or second thoughts. More than in level four, hand holding in public is natural, as well as rubbing each other's neck, hugging, kissing, and cuddling. When you see each other you greet one another with open arms, a smile and a kiss. Saying the words "I love you," "You complete me," "You're my other half" may also become natural for the two of you to say at the end of every telephone conversation. You can find yourself saying this to one another in the morning before departing and at night before going to bed. The power of these words is what holds the true authority in the relationship.

Valentine's Day will become that special day where nobody and nothing will come between the two of you. In fact, he should take the entire day off and spend it with you. From morning to sunset, that day will become "Your Day" instead of Valentine's Day. Dozens of roses, Valentine's Day cards, boxes of See's candy (the large boxes), and reservations at YOUR favorite restaurant, regardless of cost.

When you decide to open your heart to enter into this level of love you are agreeing to accept the whole man just as he is. And he is agreeing to accept the whole woman you are, just as you are. If he forgets to put the toilet seat down, it doesn't make you angry. If he forgets to take the trash out, it's okay. If he becomes unemployed and can't find employment, you've got his back and this doesn't get you angry. At this level, you are pretty much in it for keeps, and the words "In love" become "Deep Love" for you. You're unable to complain about stuff you know you can't change. It will also have you looking for the good in him and ignoring his flaws. This level of love also brings him home every night, and he's not thinking about cheating and neither are you. Of course you would love to have that man with the six figure income, benefits, retirement plan, 401K, credit cards with a high limit, and I'm not talking about some "Debit Card" that gives you the illusion that you have a credit card. He has a high FICO Score with excellent credit, his own home, and this includes having no children. That is what you call a "Dream Man." This level of love may not offer you all of the things I just mentioned, because this love comes from the inside of a man which isn't attached to some 401K or a high FICO Score. When you reach this type of love you have truly found the hidden treasure and your soul mate. This level will cause your soul mate to experience death while living, when their partner passes away. A part of your spirit leaves your body and it travels with your soul mate believe it or not.

This level also stabilizes the relationship. Did I mention unconditional love? Unconditional love cannot be purchased or found under some rock; unconditional love is what two people build together. I'm sure you're saying to yourselves that you want to be in love with someone like that. Ladies, stop looking to be "In Love" wait to find that "Deep Love." If you are, "In" something you can very well be, "Out" of it. Love running deep is what I call real, true, solid love. The deeper you fall, the harder it is for him, or you to get up, or in this case, out of it.

At this level, nothing can come between you and your partner. Your love is stronger than your pride. Everyday should be cherished by one another, when your partner kisses you it feels like a kiss of life. Every day is Christmas and every night is New Year Eve.

SIXTH LEVEL OF LOVE

Love is desired by all

This level of love is a level I wish no one has to experience in life. I call this "**Crazy Love**." This type of love will have you walking around in "La La Land" You will not know if you're coming or going, or if it's day or night. This level will control your every move; in fact, it will control your entire life. It will take you out of your character and have you worried about things you shouldn't be worried about. You can't sleep at night, can't eat, you are checking his emails, and all of his incoming, and outgoing calls from his cell phone. It can make you deliberately get pregnant so you will have a connection with him for the rest of your life.

Crazy love will also cause you to burn down houses, give away all of his clothes, pour sugar into the gas tank, break out car windows, key his brand new car, flatten his tires, stalk him, and smell his dirty underwear to see if he had sex with some other woman. Believe it or not, it can cause you to cuss your own mother out in church in front of the Preacher, if she catches you on the wrong day. Oh, before I forget, this type of love will allow you to remain in an abusive relationship until you or he either goes to prison where he can no longer hit you, or until your family and friends are standing over your gravesite wearing black, and wiping their eyes with a handkerchief.

Love doesn't ever inflict pain, it's a protector and it shields you from pain. True love never wants to say good-bye. 9-1-1 is only three buttons away.

Don't become a victim to an abusive love relationship.

Chapter Three

Power of the V Wisdom

Knowing my daughter like I do, she's on her way home to prepare to deal with her hot-headed boyfriend whenever he decides to return home. Dominece, with her strong personality, isn't going to take much more of these so-called games her boyfriend is playing.

She told me later what happened after she left the house.

She told me that she connected her iPod. She cranked the volume as loud as it could go, and waited for Mary J Blige's song, "Fine," to play. She sang along as the song played, burning rubber as she drove off.

Dominece pulled into her parking spot and headed down the walkway to her apartment. She walked into her house, throwing her purse and house keys down on a nearby end table. As she made her way through the living room toward her bedroom, a male's voice shouted out, "Where have you been?"

Dominece stopped, turned around and said, "None of your damn business." The male voice didn't respond, and she kept walking. AJ sat in the dark room alone.

After a few seconds passed he yelled, "What do you mean, none of my damn business. And where is my son's?"

"*Our* sons is with my dad." Dominece made her way to the bedroom and called it a night.

THREE WEEKS LATER

"Baby, it's been three weeks since you and I have had sex," says AJ.

"Really? I haven't notice the time. Man, how time flies when you're not having sex," said Dominece, smiling.

"I'm tired of playing these games with you. So when can I have some?"

"Some what?" Dominece asked as she continued to watch television.

"Sex, Baby. Sex."

"That may be a while. See, I had a talk with my dad, and he explained to me how I have the power, and not you. Now I understand my worth and my value. You need to catch up."

AJ walked around behind Dominece and placed his arms around her neck, and whispered something sweet in her ear, while kissing her neck. As much as she tried to resist AJ's advances, she ultimately gave in.

"Come on baby. Let Big Papa rock your world. You know how good I put it down, and you know you want it just as bad as I do." AJ picked Dominece up and took her into the bedroom.

My daughter was another statistic. She, like many women, fell for a man's empty words, completely ignoring the fact that this man still doesn't have a job to support her or their two kids. She is ignoring the reality that he is using her.

AJ is no different than millions of other men out there that find their way into a woman's life, and uses them for whatever they can get. When these men finish using women as much as they can, and they have taken all there is to take, they move on to the next victim. The sad thing is many of these young and sometimes older women never see it coming. If they would simply open their eyes, maybe they would see the game that is being played, and avoid a world of hurt. Instead they settle for someone who only pretends to love them.

I believe that a woman will fall in love with a man much faster than a man will fall in love with a woman. I'm not saying that this is impossible, but, it is not likely. I believe it takes a man's feelings longer to connect with a woman's. Through my experiences when I was younger, I have had one or two women tell me that they were in love with me within seven days. I thought it was a little too quick for me because I could not understand how a person could love someone so quickly. It wasn't until I got older and started to pay attention to the differences in how females interact in comparison to males. I cannot say that my daughter's boyfriend is like the men I described because I don't know him, but my daughter seems to feel that he's a good man, and a pretty good father, which, I suppose, means a lot to women with children.

This is why it's important for females of all ages to truly understand their worth and value in order to realize their true power. Women should take notice of the manipulation game that is played while they're in a relationship with a man who refuses to make any type of contribution in the household. If he makes no attempt to find work to support his family, especially when kids are involved, he is less than a man. Just because he has a penis doesn't make him a man, and just because he's over the age of twenty-one doesn't mean he knows what it takes to be a man. What makes a *real* man is a man who recognizes his shortcomings and does something about them. A real man understands his responsibilities, and makes sacrifices, and does the work to support himself without the help of anyone else. A man should want to enter into a relationship with something more to offer than a hard penis and a wet tongue.

Women and men have to accept that there isn't much that a parent can do once their daughter turns a certain age, starts to engage in sexual activities and begins having her own family. When something like this takes place neither a mother nor father can take the place of what a man (or boy) is giving their daughter. This is why so many young women get into arguments with their mothers. I watched it happen with my five sisters and our mother. It also happened between my oldest daughter and her mother. These young women begin to feel and act as though they are grown women.

As a parent there is only so much we can teach our children. We can share the mistakes that we made when we were their age. Either they listen and learn, or they decide not to listen, and go out and make their own mistakes. I can only hope that what I told her didn't go in one ear and out of the other, but only time will tell. True wisdom should never fall on deaf ears, but of course, this new generation has a mind of its own.

We wish and hope for the best for our children. We dream of things for them like college, career, marriage, owning a home, and then having children, especially if it's your daughter. The thought of your young baby girl having sex with some silly boy, and knowing that he probably doesn't have a pot to piss in or a window to throw it out of is painful.

Women today make decisions about their bodies and their lives believing that they don't have many—or any—real choices when it comes to the men in their lives. I'm not saying there aren't any good men out there. However, what I am saying is, finding a decent man is like looking for a needle in a haystack.

Luckily for Dominece, the next day after she gave in to AJ's advances, AJ sold his X-Box, got rid of all his video games, and found himself a part-time job at a local car wash. A month later they were married in Vegas. Today, Dominece and AJ have had their third child.

It appears that my daughter found her power before things got too out of hand, and she was able to gain control over her relationship. Unlike many others whose relationships lead to abuse or death, Dominece was able to avoid that horrible outcome. I like to think that sharing my knowledge with her helped her avoid a tragic outcome. In many relationships whether young, or old, a turn for the worse can occur when a person does not know how to handle certain situations. It isn't about how much fun you have with your partner, or how good you think the sex is. It's more about knowing how to maintain a healthy relationship. Take this story and use it as a guide for those of you who are still searching for a companion. Knowing who you are is the first step to getting to know your partner. Self-understanding is the essential key in order to understand anyone else.

I will go as far as to say that my daughter went from a level one love relationship, to a level four relationship without knowing how or when she got there. One of the mistakes I noticed my daughter made was that she gave AJ everything she had without any expectations from him. Due to the recession, I'd be a fool to think that my daughter could get lucky and end up with a millionaire. This doesn't mean that she has to settle for anything less than a relationship based upon love, respect, loyalty and equality. A man is supposed to lift his woman up, not keep her down, and this includes keeping her safe. What happened to the sense of responsibility that we men are supposed to have?

The V wisdom has been shared, and now I will wait and see what my daughter will do with it. I just hope she doesn't use this wisdom as a form of punishment like some women do. When an argument occurs between her and her mate, I hope that she truly realizes that she holds the power, and does not allow her weakness to separate her from the knowledge of the V power she now holds. Again, knowledge can only be shared and not forced on anyone. "You can lead a horse to water, but you can't make him drink." In other words, there is only so much we can do as parents. The rest is up to our children. We must raise our young girls to be aware of what will be expected of them as an adult. However, there is no guarantee that what we attempt to instill in our young ladies as we teach them how to become powerful women will come to fruition.

Chapter Four

Women Hold the Power

ONE WEEK LATER

My daughter, Dominece, and a group of her girlfriends met for dinner at a restaurant one week from the day she and AJ made up. Apparently, she wanted to share what she had learned from me with her friends. It felt good knowing that she wanted to share her new found wisdom with her women friends. *Reach one; teach one* is what we all should do. This is a story of a young woman who feels the need to protect her friends from any mentally or physically abusive relationships like the one she experienced first-hand.

"What are you talking about, Dominece? Spit it out. I'm not in the mood to play these guessing games with you!" said Debra, a 23-year-old single mother of one, who is very out spoken and sassy.

"I'm talking about our vaginas, believe it or not," Dominece answers.

"Vaginas! You brought us here to talk about our vaginas?" 'Shelly, who is a 20-year-old single woman with an attitude,' asked Dominece.

"Yes! I brought you all here to talk about our V's. This is something that we really don't talk about these days and I wonder why? I think it's important to talk about the vagina, and the power we think it holds. Many of us have used it incorrectly." said Dominece.

"I used *my* stuff to my advantage." Shelly says.

"So, Dominece, what are you thinking we should we do with this power we possess?" Connie asks, a 22-year-old single working woman, mother of two.

"For starters, we should expect more than what have already been given. The day we realize that our V's belong to *us* and not our men, will be the day we come to understand the real power. Women desire companionship, but men need intimacy, which includes the vagina." Dominece replies.

"Take the vagina out of the equation and the chase stops. Men chase us for one thing, and one thing only," said Sandi, a 19-year-old single woman, with wisdom of a 70-year-old woman.

"I've been taught, by my Granny that, a woman should surrender herself only to her husband." said Dorothy, a 25 year old Christian woman, who believes in having strong morals and values.

"Amen!" said Connie.

"Sex has become over-rated these days. Sex is now being used to sell cars and hamburgers. You remember the Carl's Jr commercial where Paris Hilton was rolling all over the car while washing it, with a huge hamburger in her hands? This is what media and society really think of women," said Connie.

Donna, a 17 year-old shy, single woman with no children who believes in marriage first then sex, says, "It's not like men can walk into Wal-Mart and buy a piece on aisle four near the garden tools."

Everyone laughs out loud.

When we look back at these uninformed young women that suffer from lack of education regarding relationships, men, sex, control, and power, we can't help but say to ourselves: Why isn't there a course that teaches women about self-control and the power that they possess. Take the commercial with Paris Hilton. Was it necessary for her or any other woman to promote a $6 hamburger that way? I don't know about you, but I think that a good hamburger sells itself. It goes back to a woman knowing her self-worth, and standing firm in her convictions about how she wants to be treated, and perceived.

These young ladies appear to be thirsty for power, knowledge and wisdom, but they need to do a little research about the meaning of power, first. When you look up the word "power," it means, "to control." Control over one, *not* another human being. The power of the vagina can be—and often *is*—misused. Having this power gives no one the right to use it to control or manipulate.

Do women hold the power? Now think of any major sports star you've read about in the last few years that were caught in sex scandals. Now, think of the when, the where, and the "who" they shouldn't have been with. The vagina is so powerful that immature men have allowed themselves to become weak because of it. This proves just how strong the vagina is. Some would say that they fell weak for another woman; I believe he fell short for the vagina and only the vagina. All immature men say, "I have let my family down, and

I regret those transgressions with all of my heart." Or they say, "I am dealing with my behavior and personal failings behind closed doors with my family. Those feelings should be shared by us alone." These statements should not be made publicly, but to their wives, and families privately. When a man creeps around with another woman and he's married, it's only for one thing and one thing only: The vagina.

The women involved in these scandals are no less to blame. These women are engaging in sexual intercourse with someone that they know is married with a family. Do I blame the women who get involved with these rich and powerful men? No, I do not. I blame the men. The men are married, which means they have an obligation to their wives, and their family to keep it in their pants, and to control their urges, period. Many people feel that because these men are rich and powerful, they are Gods. Well, I don't feel that way, in my opinion, a man is just a man, like any other man. These men just happen to have money and fame. Many have stated that, without the money, and fame most of these men would have never committed adultery. Maybe . . . . maybe not. I personally think that if a man has the largest mansion in the state, several luxury cars, fame, millions of dollars, and just happens to be married he thinks he's untouchable. He feels as if he doesn't have to follow a moral path. He assumes a sense of entitlement.

If you are not ready to eat your favorite flavor of ice cream for the rest of your life, when asked to say "I do." say, "I don't!"

For these famous sports players, when the smoke clears, they are all going to have to look in the mirror and ask themselves one question: "Was she worth it?"

The women after men of this status need to find their power of the V. They need to restrain themselves from being in a committed relationship until they actually know their value. I agree with the Late James Brown. "This world wouldn't be anything without a woman or a girl."

So when we see a woman or a girl, we should see their self-respect and honor first. It's really not about a woman or a girl having the power. It's more about men understanding what a woman truly brings to our society, our homes, our work places, etc. Women need to understand what they bring to our lives and cherish their power of the V.

Chapter Five

The V and High School Boys

There is a group of teenage girls hanging out after school around the high school boy's gym; they are watching some twelfth grade boys practice for an upcoming basketball game. Brandy and Susan are 15 years old, Tina is 16, and Jessica is 17. The girls are sitting on the bleachers sharing their sexual experiences with one another. It appears that watching young sweaty high school boys play basketball is more important than getting home to do homework or studying.

"I like that jump shot, Jimmy!" Tina jumps up and shouts when Jimmy makes a shot from the three-point line.

"Girl, will you sit your butt down," Jessica says as she pulls Tina by the sleeve.

"Every time Jimmy makes a shot, she jumps up like she's some cheerleader rooting for her favorite team," Susan says.

"You guys are jealous because Jimmy and I did it," Tina replies.

"What? You and Jimmy are screwing? I didn't know that," Susan says.

"Neither did I?" says Jessica.

"And neither did I. I'm always the last to hear about these things," Brandy adds.

"I thought I told you girls that Jimmy and I are messing around. It's been about two months now." Tina says as she smiles from ear to ear.

"No, you didn't tell your best friends that you and the All Star Basketball Player were screwing one another," Jessica says.

"Well, I'm sure you're not the only one screwing Jimmy Boy. I heard that he was messing with three other girls," Brandy says.

"You can't believe everything your ears hear or everything your eyes see." Tina says as she rolls her eyes.

"I don't believe everything my ears hear, but I can't help but believe my own eyes, especially when I saw it for myself," Brandy says.

"Spill it, Brandy. What did you see?" Jessica asks.

Brandy leans in closer to the girls and whispers, "It was last Friday during lunch break. I saw Jimmy and some freshman going into the men's restroom."

Tina interrupts Brandy's story with, "That doesn't mean Jimmy did anything with her."

Brandy ignores the interruption and continues, "Anyways, I snuck in after them and the two of them were in one of the stalls. The girl was on her knees and Jimmy was making all kinds of noises, if you know what I mean."

Tina, not wanting to give ground says, "that don't mean nuthin'. Jimmy doesn't care about anyone but me. In fact, I was in the stall with Jimmy just the other day. So what!" Tina says.

"WHAT?" Jessica shouts out as she stands up and looks at Tina.

"Sit down, Jessica. The only difference between you and Tina is that Tina used a restroom stall, and you used the classroom closet to give Michael oral sex.

If I'm not mistaken, you had sex with Michael not so long ago. So, sit down."
Susan says.

Jessica, fires back, "Look who's talking. I caught you and Gary doing it in
the back of his car. Remember?" Tina, Jessica and Susan all turn around and
look at Brandy, as she attempts to look innocent.

"What?" Brandy asks the girls.

"You're not a virgin so don't judge us." Susan says.

Annoyed, Brandy says, "I never said I was a virgin. My hormones got the
best of me when I was in elementary school. I think I was ten or eleven when
I lost my virginity to my first crush."

"Damn! Ten?" Susan screams out.

"Face it girls, we all have done things we know we probably shouldn't have."
Tina says.

"Brandy, why so young?" Jessica asks.

"Peer pressure mostly," one of my friends lost her virginity when she was
nine, and five of her friends had already lost their virginity, so the pressure of
wanting to fit in got the best of me. I went and let her older brother take my
virginity," Brandy says.

"How old was your friend's brother?" Susan asks.

Not really wanting to tell her friends the answer, Brandy hesitates but finally
blurts out, "He was seventeen."

"SEVENTEEN?" Jessica shouts out as she stands up and placed her hands
on her hips.

"See, I knew you were going to react that way. I should never have told you
that. Ok, so I knew he was too old for me, and I shouldn't have done it, but that
was then and this is now. If it wasn't someone seventeen it would have been
someone closer to my age, so what's the difference? I lost my virginity. What's
done is done," Brandy says.

"Do you regret it?" Tina asks Brandy

"No. Do you regret it?" Brandy asks Tina.

Tina thinks for a moment and then tells the group, "No, not at all. I love the way sex makes me feel, before doing it, while I'm doing it, and after I've done it."

"What about you, Susan, do you regret losing your virginity?" Tina asked.

"Nope, my mother was in her teens when she gave birth to me. She lost her virginity at the age of twelve. Look, neither one of us have fathers in the home. In fact, I have never even seen my father. There is no one in my home to teach me about sex. My mother works two jobs trying to keep a roof over our heads, which pretty much leaves me to raise myself. This is my life and it is what it is." Susan says.

When I hear stories like this, it saddens me. Where are the fathers in all of their lives? We as fathers have an obligation to these young women and not just a financial obligation. We also have an obligation to teach, guide our daughters, and to protect them from making mistakes like this.

Today there's a new breed of girls growing up in our world. By the time they turn thirteen, they are already beginning their journey toward womanhood trying to create adult relationships, becoming sexually promiscuous in an attempt to develop self-esteem. Peer pressure, raging hormones and lack of sexual experience cause many young women to choose a path that is taking them away from the power of their V, and from more important things like their education.

I believe that once a girl has sex, particularly if the experience was a positive one, it is much more difficult to tell her to stop having sex. Parents need to instill in their daughters self-respect and self-control before they take that giant step into sexual activity. Preventing it from happening is easier than trying to convince them after the fact. Billions of people are addicted to chocolate, and to this generation, sex is like chocolate. It has become an addiction.

In the story above, these four teenage girls are without a father in the home and/or a positive male influence in their lives. They also have mother's that believe working to pay the bills is more important than teaching their daughters how to avoid the same mistakes some of them made regarding sex. We need to obligate ourselves as parents, mothers, fathers, grandmothers, grandfathers, and others to teach our teenage girls that they hold the power of their V. They have the power of self-control and self esteem. It really does take a village to raise a child.

We must teach our daughters how to avoid being manipulated by their male peers. For example, ladies, if a young boy walks up to a girl and says to her, "I love you, baby," that doesn't mean he wants to marry you, I assure you. What it *really* means is "Give me some."

In other words: Boys lie, period. Oh, they'll tell you they aren't lying, but let me assure you, they are lying through their teeth. If they're still in high school, they don't know what real love is. If they don't have a steady, legal job, they don't know what real love is. They only want to get you on your back. And that's a fact.

Don't fall for their manipulation. They lie because they love friction. It's nothing more, nothing less. Older men lie too, but for reasons besides friction.

Lust and love are two different things. Stop mistaking one for the other. One steals your V power and the other enhances it. What these girls and millions of girls don't know is, that a boy's lies can have serious consequences. You can get a venereal disease, or worse, pregnant. Now, who's going to take care of you and your baby? Not him, I guarantee it. You'll be on your own, or you'll become an added burden to your family. You need to understand your power of the V. If you don't, you won't be ready for a sexual relationship. Learn the V power listen to your mind, that still, small voice, ignore everything else.

To all young girls, listen up, your raging female hormones have a voice. She can talk to you. She can make you do dumb things. She is not your friend. She's looking to become friends with male hormones. You teenage girls have to face the fact that you've only been on this planet for 14 to 17 years, and the first three years many of you were in diapers, learning your "ABC's." Those were your cognitive years. Everything in life is a learning process. You are just not ready mentally. You are not equipped, or experienced enough to deal with a relationship that includes the V.

Many teenage relationships look like they're going somewhere and they turn out to be a nightmare. Here are a few things to remember while engaged in that type of a relationship:

1. If a man ever calls you a "bitch," you call him "GONE!"

2. Never become a man's punching bag. Once a punching bag, always a punching bag! Don't blame him if you stay; blame yourself, because you allowed it to happen.

3. If he has kids by another woman and he doesn't take care of them, this is usually a sign that a man is not responsible. If he won't take care of his, then he won't take care of yours. Don't waste your time.

4. Don't get mad at your man, GET OUT!

5. "Aretha had it right: R-E-S-P-E-C-T." Without it you don't have a real relationship.

Chapter Six

God's Gift to Women

Summer 2009. Sandi and her boyfriend, Pretty Slim, have lived together for nine months, and decided to take a trip to Las Vegas for three days. While sitting at the piano bar in the hotel, Sandi decided to bring up the conversation of V power with Pretty Slim. Slim is an ex-pimp who ran a crew of street prostitutes in Los Angeles back in the early eighties. Sandi had no idea what she was getting herself into. The smooth, slick words that came out of Slims mouth were enough to gain the attention of Sandi and later those same words captured her heart, and, ultimately almost destroyed her.

Of course, within weeks, Slim was living with Sandi, eating her out of house and home, and driving her car. For Slim, it proved that he still had the magic touch, the touch that can get a woman to say "yes" to anything he asks for, and "no" to the things he doesn't want her to do. Poor Sandi, it would be the beginning of the end for her, and a crude revelation finding out the truth about Slim. Sandi's story is that of a woman who wants to know if her man knows her true worth, and that she is a gift from God.

"Honey, the girls and I got together last week at Friday's for dinner, and drinks, anyway my girl, Dominica, started a conversation about sex, men and power."

"Why would you of all people get together with a group of chicken heads to discuss sex, men and power when you got a man to talk to about that?"

"What do you mean chicken heads? They're my girlfriends."

"When I see your girlfriends, I see chicken heads," Pretty Slim responded.

"And when I see your homeboys I see losers, and as far as us discussing sex, men and power, the conversation wasn't actually directed at me. It was a question being asked, so we all answered. I wanted to ask you your thoughts about the vagina, since you were a pimp back in the day with a flock of chicks walking up and down the street."

"I feel as though the woman is the most perfect creature ever created, if you ask me. But, your vagina is no more than a hole. That is what I think about all V's, including my mamas. She's no different."

"How dare you compare your mother to every stinking 'ho' you been with in your lifetime. Have you ever loved anybody other than yourself? You arrogant jerk. That is why when you told me you loved me I never believed you. Until you are able to love a woman as much as you love yourself, you will never find love, and if you are lucky enough to find it you still won't recognize it, because love to you is not spelled the way everyone else spells it. To you "love" is spelled S-e-l-f."

"You know what your problem is?" says Pretty Slim, "You're trying to give your V too much power. It has no power, as far as I'm concerned."

"How did it make you feel when you had all those women standing on street corners selling their precious bodies and bringing you the money? Did it make you feel like the 'man?' Did it give you the power you needed on the streets? Did it give you street creditability?"

Pretty Slim sat there with his mouth wide open as he listened to his girlfriend go on, and on about him misusing women, and about how he used to pimp back in the days.

Sandi could have talked until her face turned blue. It didn't matter what she said or how she said it. Pretty Slim was once a pimp, and that is a fact that she nor anyone else will ever change. Most pimps don't break their style or swagger very easily. It usually becomes a way of life for them.

It took Sandi nine months to kick Slim out of her of her home. She had to call the police one evening to have Slim removed from her house, because he refused to leave.

This story clearly demonstrates a woman that feels that she is so in need of a man that she lets her guard down. She allows not just an ordinary man, but an ex-pimp to come into her life and into her home. Pretty Slim grew up caring nothing about a woman except for what she can do for him. Sandi's mistake was that she never asked Slim important questions before getting into a relationship with him which would have allowed her to make a better decision. Most times, a woman that is not accustomed to being in a relationship with a man tries to avoid asking too many questions. She really might not want to hear his answers. She doesn't want to hear anything bad, especially after she has gone out with him a few times. In her mind, she wants him to be Mr. Right.

Many women that seem as if they are desperate to be in a relationship usually make this same mistake. They ignore all of the warning signs, like the pushing her against the wall, and later he says he's sorry; or I was just teasing. What about when he raises his voice at you for no reason at all? When you enter into a relationship and the only thing that is open is your heart and not your eyes, it's difficult to really see what you're getting yourself into. Keep your eyes open and your ears un-plugged, most of the time you will avoid wasting time with a good-for-nothing man. Talk less and listen more when you are out with a man. If you listen long enough, he will tell you everything there is to know about him.

The saying is, "to tell if a man is a good man, look at the way he treats his mother". Well, apparently, my girl Sandi never heard that cliché because if she did, I am almost certain that she never would have gotten involved with Pretty Slim.

Was it Pretty Slims' fault? No, this mistake falls solely on Sandi's shoulders. Slim was just being himself. She thought his swagger was cute and that the way he spoke was smooth. Like many women, she got caught up in the web of deceit. When a man builds his personality and character around those he admires attempting to change him will be impossible. Character most time than not doesn't change, and it usually can't be replaced. You can take a man out of the country, but you can't take the country out of the man. The same goes for Pretty Slim. Except in this case, you can't make a pimp into a husband.

Not all pimps have on large hats tilted with feathers on the side, and they are not wearing red seven-inch platform shoes and a perm in their hair. Being a pimp is more about being able to manipulate the mind of another human being. It is not all about running a stable of women.

So ladies, remember, once a pimp always a pimp. So don't sit around waiting to be pimped.

Chapter Seven

Controlling the V Power

Back at Shelly's house, she's arguing with her ex-boyfriend and her baby's daddy, James.

James thinks he can walk in and out of her life. He demands to have sex with her any time he wants to, because he was her first, and he's the father of her only son. He's standing at her front door in a pair of blue jeans, a white T-shirt, a pair of Air Jordan tennis shoes, with a blue baseball cap on his head turned backwards. Most women give in to a man's request, especially if they're not in a relationship with anyone else and they feel the need to be held by a man.

Here is a story about a man believing he's God's gift to woman, but he's about to find out that he's just another man.

The doorbell rings, Shelly goes to the front door to see who it is. She opens the door and James is standing there with his hands in his pocket. Shelly is in disbelief.

"What do you want, James? Your son is at my mom's house for the weekend. He will be back on Sunday if you are here to visit him."

"I didn't come by here to see my son; I came by here to see you. It's been a minute for us, so I thought it was time for a brotha to tap that thing. You know how we used to do it, baby girl."

"I do remember how we used to do it, but those days are behind us James. I have moved on with my life."

"How are you going to stand there in my face, and tell your baby's daddy that you have moved on with your life? Come on, girl. Let me tap that one more time, for old time's sake. Remember, I was your first and I'll always be your last."

"No. You have a new woman, go get what you want from her and leave me the hell alone." said Shelly.

"What do you mean 'no'? So what if I have another woman. You're mine and you always will be. What's between those legs is mine anytime I want it. I should slap you, woman." James said as he raised his right hand up at Shelly.

Shelly turns her face and raises her arm up to protect herself from being hit.

Respect, honesty, faithfulness, love, kind words, a few dinners, a couple of concerts, was all Shelly wanted from James.

Unfortunately, this story is typical. There are many men that believe when they are the woman's first, they will be her last, or when kids are involved, that gives them the right to the woman's vagina for as long as she lives. Men that think like that need to look at the bigger picture, which is: If he was a responsible father to his son, with a job and had shown more respect to the woman in his life, he wouldn't be standing at the front door asking Shelly to, "Let me hit that one more time for old time sake." Shelly would still be his woman and not his ex-.

Poor Shelly, she told me that she allowed James to have his way with her for a long time. She overlooked the fact that he gave her several venereal diseases. Shelly allowed this man to beat her as if she was one of his' enemies. That wasn't all. She sat back and let him disrespect her in front of his homeboys, and his mother. Just when I thought I had heard enough, she tells me that this man stole from her causing her and their three year old son to be evicted not once, but twice. She was extremely foolish in this relationship, but I can only hope that days like those are behind her, and that she can move on with her life without James.

James had a control issue. He felt and acted as though he owned Shelly, and what was between her legs. I will assume that Shelly told James once, twice or maybe a few times that he had it going on in the bedroom. Why else would James think that he has the right to come in and out of her life without any type of regard for her feelings? I have seen this type of relationship, where the man clearly controls the woman's every move. If he says jump, she will ask how high. A manipulated mind, or a beating, controls that type of relationship. There are men out there who believe if they put fear in a woman she will do whatever it is he wants her to do. After talking with Shelly, it appeared that she was ready to take back the life and the courage that James stole from her.

No one can be controlled by anyone unless that person allows it to happen, whether it is a male or female. Remember, to control someone, is to have power over them. Power or control can never be taken or stolen. Power and control are given to the controller through fear or manipulation.

Let Shelly's experience be a lesson for you. How much control are you willing to allow a man to have over you? How, many times do you have to visit a medical clinic or hospital before you decide that enough is enough? How many times do you have to be raped in order to get the message that he's trying to break your spirit. You are allowing that individual to take what little strength you have left away from you. His plan is for you to become solely dependent on him.

"I control you. I tell you when it's over. You belong to me," said James as he stared at Shelly.

Shelly allowed herself to remain in a relationship with a man that did not deserve her love. She is like millions of other young women who get pregnant and hope that the man will marry them. They do not consider the possibility that their partner is not ready to assume the responsibility of being a father or provider. This is another example of how some women accept any man that comes along without asking him any questions about his life.

What many women don't know is that most men's brains are wired to have compulsive sex. In most cases women's brains are not, which means some women can do without sex much longer than their male companion. Women that know men's brains are 'wired to their sexual mid-brain' have an advantage over men. This allows the female to become dominate in the relationship, when it comes to sexual intercourse. Men allow sex to become a need for them and most women think of as sex as pleasure. Ideally, you want to be in a relationship with someone who treats you as an equal, and treats you with love, kindness and respect.

Today women seem fine with accepting a part of a man whereas before they wouldn't accept anything less than the whole man. Which brings me to another question: Why are so many women today willing to share a man? When I spoke to a female friend of mine she stated that the competition has become so fierce, that women are playing the "Pick Me" game with men. "If you pick me, I'll let you drive my car while I'm at work," "If you pick me, you can live with me without paying any bills." "If you pick me, I'll pay your bills." If you pick me, you can date other women as long as you come home to me every night." Even though plenty of women may not come straight out and say these exact words. Believe me, that is the message that is being sent to men. It is becoming known as an "Open Invitation" for men to treat their women badly.

When you accept this type of behavior, you're giving up what little power you have and turning it over to the man. What I have never understood is why would a woman give 100% and accept 20% in return? The young woman, Shelly, experienced this with her ex-boyfriend, James. That was one of the reasons why Shelly broke up with James. The second reason was he cheated. What I have found to be true is that once a man cheats, and a woman takes him back, the chance of him cheating again becomes much greater. He figures if you forgave him and accepted him back once, you'll do it again. Cheating is lying. Where there are lies, there can't be trust, and where there is no trust, there cannot be any type of real relationship.

Control is a funny thing, but it is possible to be in control when you're stable and have control over yourself. To control is to take charge and many people fear being in charge of their own life. If you are not in control of yourself then you can never have control over your V. When you discover your control you will find the true person that lives within you.

Chapter Eight

Easy V

The title of this chapter is self-explanatory. It's about a female co-worker that has slept with every man she works with. There has to be something seriously wrong for anyone to deliberately have sex with thirty-six men within two months. Here's the story about one woman that gives new meaning to the word 'easy.' Try to keep an open mind while reading her story.

"You're not going to believe who I had sex with last night." Said a middle-aged guy named Joe.

"Who?" Billy asked as they talked on the telephone.

"Susan from work."

"Susan? That's nothing new. I've had Susan many times and so did half of the other guys who work there. You're probably the last guy to get some. Susan gives away vagina like a store going out of business. It's a free for all. She makes it easy to get it."

"Seriously?"

"Trust me. Everyone that passes through her front door gets exactly the same thing."

"Oh, man! I feel like a sucker."

"Joe, you've done nothing wrong."

"I should have known. It was the easiest piece of tail I've ever got. I didn't have to do anything, or say much, she just gave it up. I wonder why she is going around giving it up that easily."

Joe is no different than millions of other men. He saw an opportunity to get laid so he took advantage of it. There's nothing like some free vagina, except that you might come away with an STD.

I believe many women like Susan offer themselves to men for self pleasure or in some cases, to please the man in hopes of finding love. Some of the women I have spoken with, especially younger women believe that the sooner they give themselves to a man, the sooner he will grow to love them. I really do not believe that women go around having sex with men just for the hell of it. Having no father or a male figure in the home can cause a woman to grow up looking for the father they never had. If fathers were in the household spending quality time, and showing their daughter attention, love wouldn't be an issue when they become older. Everyone has a purpose, and this is a prime example of why our daughters need to be taught at an early age. They need to be educated about how important it is to hold on to their value and self-worth.

When looking back on this story, Susan could very well have been addicted to sex or suffering from low self-esteem. She needs to seek help from a professional. However, anyone experiencing this type of addiction must first be made aware of their addiction, and be willing to admit that there is a problem. Trying to gain the attention of a man by using your body, hardly ever works in your favor. The only advice I can offer Susan or anyone else out there that exhibits this type of behavior is: One, find yourself. Start with being celibate for six months to a year. Find a healthy replacement for sex and men. Two, in order to re-build your self-esteem, you must know your value, and worth as a woman and never think of yourself as "less than." Validation does not have to come from someone else or by getting nominated for a Hollywood award. Most actors feel validated when they win an Oscar, when, in fact, if you're a great actor, it doesn't matter whether you win or lose if you get nominated. There can only be one winner based in the category, but does this mean that the other five actors weren't good or great? Of course it doesn't. Validation starts from within and it expresses itself outwardly. Study yourself, don't become an easy catch, an easy screw or allow yourself to become labeled as an easy vagina.

Chapter Nine

Poor Girl's V

While many people struggle to get out of housing projects, there are some that have become comfortable with their living conditions and refuse to leave—or even believe that they can leave.

Take this story about a middle-aged African American woman, Nikki and her 14-year-old daughter, Simone. Nikki, a single mother of five, grew up on the East Side of Los Angeles, California in a low-income area. Nikki feels that she cannot do any better with her life. In spite of everything, Nikki's daughter Simone is determined to make a better life for herself by any means necessary.

On a Saturday afternoon, Nikki and Simone are standing at a nearby bus stop waiting for the bus to arrive. They are on the way to the shopping mall which is located twenty miles from where they live.

After a few moments, Simone breaks the silence, "Hey Mama, when are you going to sit down with me and teach me about boys and sex?"

"BOYS AND SEX? Are you planning to have sex with someone?" asks Nikki as she looks Simone in the eye.

Simone looks away from her mother and says, "I didn't want to tell you because I knew you would get mad at me."

"Are you kidding me?"

Still averting her mother's stare, Simone whispers, "No."

"I'll be damned! I thought for sure you being my last child, that you would wait at least until you were eighteen, not fourteen."

"So, Mama, what do I need to know about boys and sex?" says Simone.

"There's nothing to know. Boy meets girl, girl says yes, boy climbs on top of girl, boy feels good, and boy get's up and goes home. That's the real education about boys and sex," says Nikki.

"Is that it?"

"That's it baby."

"Okay, Mama. Well, a boy at school offered me two hundred dollars to have sex with him," Simone blurts out.

Nikki nearly chokes when she hears her daughter say this. "You're talking like a cheap whore now."

"What about the men you got running in and out of our house mama? I'm sure they're not coming over to fix the toilet."

"You better watch your mouth and mind your own business. The men I bring over to my house are my friends. Besides, once in a while they do take mama to the ninety-nine cent store, and spend a few dollars on food for you, and your sisters. I don't need much, and poor girls can't charge much for their coochie anyway."

"You may not need much, but Bree, Tonya, Pam, Tina and I, need some new clothes, and I'm tired of going to bed hungry."

"Those men don't owe you or me a penny. They're not your father, and they have no plans on playing the 'Baby daddy' role. Poor girls are just happy to get laid from time to time. If we try to charge men for sex, shit, we might not ever get laid. Lord knows the men from our hood ain't got a pot to piss in, or a window to throw it out of. We're poor girls, Simone, and poor girls usually have to settle for crumbs. Most men with money don't look at us the same way that they look at other women from the West Side. They expect us poor girls to give it up for free."

"I'm tired of being poor," Simone mutters.

Nikki holds her daughter tightly and says; "It's okay baby. I know how you feel. Mama has been poor all her life and it don't look like anything is going to come my way to change that. I suppose the saying is true, 'Life is a bitch and then you die.'"

Simone looks up at her mother and says; "So you think I should wait until I'm married first before having sex?"

"I got five kids by five different men. I don't know anybody in the project who's married to his or her baby's daddy. Life ain't some fairy tale where some rich man rides into the project on a white horse, finds a poor girl, and takes her off marries her, and then they live happily after ever. Yeah right."

It broke my heart when I heard this story. How could a mother say these things to her daughter? How can the thought of being 'poor' be deprogrammed from the mind? An individual can definitely be 'broke,' but remember, anything broken can be fixed. It should never come to a point where a young girl feels that she has no other choice except to sell her precious body, in order to put clothes on her back, or food in her stomach.

It's a fact that many low income women and girls feel as if there is no way out of poverty for them; with that being said, luckily, the above story does not speak for all low income women or girls.

It is impossible to instill hopeful thoughts and self-respect when you have little hope or self respect. In this case, Nikki does not know any better, which is why she is unable to instruct her daughter and set her on the right path. Many poor women use their financial situation to drive them, in a positive way, to conquer the challenges in their lives. If you believe that you're poor, than take the word "poor" and use it as a stepping-stone. Refuse to be poor in your thoughts, refuse to accept "no" for an answer when you believe that the answer should be "yes." To all my poor girls, know that you are only what you believe you are.

When I was growing up, my mother was on welfare and my father didn't work. I have two brothers, and five sisters, not once did any of my sisters suggest to our mother that they sell their body for money. Even though we were broke, and believe me, we were really broke, my mother taught my sisters to stay in school, get an education, and wait on a husband before having sex, because a man doesn't want a whore.

Again, this must be taught in the home, not in school or on the street corners. Was it wrong for Simone to consider losing her virginity in exchange for two hundred dollars? Yes, and no. Yes, she was wrong for even thinking about having sex at her age. No, because I understand her reasoning. She is poor and lives in a poor neighborhood and there is little or no food on the table. When you go to bed hungry some nights your dreams are about running down an alley trying to make it to school early enough to have free breakfast. Do I agree with her reasoning? No, but again, I can relate, and I understand why she would consider doing something like that.

In this illustration, notice there is no father or positive male figure in the household or in their lives. That could make a big difference. But, this depends on the male, and what it is that he teaches his children. A dead-beat dad is like the paint on the wall. Can that paint on the wall pay a bill, or put food on the table? Absolutely not! Therefore, having a man around the home isn't enough, especially if he is not contributing anything.

There are a lot of Simone's in the world who have considered selling their precious bodies because of what they don't have or wish they had. It should never reach a point where any girl or woman feels that they have to sell themselves for money, food or clothing.

I witnessed one of my nieces in the process of trading her body in exchange for cash. When I spoke to her about what she was doing, her comment was, "My mother is on welfare, the money she gets she uses it to support her habit, so I have no other choice. So I do what I do to survive in these streets, I didn't choose this life, it chose me." So what do you say to a teenager that is trying figure out what life is about? A teenage that sees nothing wrong with what she is doing? Usually guilt convinces people that what they are doing is wrong or a sin, it does nothing for those that feel they have an excuse to do wrong.

Poor women should not believe that they have no value or that they should be treated poorly. Unfortunately, many poor women can't get past thinking that they are somehow "less than" wealthier women. Change will come when poor women can replace the word "poor" with the more temporary word, "broke." As I stated earlier, anything that's broke can be fixed. I say to the poor women and girls, just because your current finances do not provide you and yours with the monetary relief that you need, know that there is always a way out. It starts with believing in yourself and your self-worth. Remember, don't make excuses to go out and sacrifice your body because of your circumstances.

It's necessary for us as parents to teach our daughters that they are worth more than material things and that just because you are on welfare doesn't mean you are poor. It just means you're temporarily without. Regardless of whether you are rich or poor, always love, respect and value yourself.

Chapter Ten

Rich Girl's V

While low, and middle class women look at their vagina as a tool to satisfy their mate while in a relationship. Rich women look at their vagina as a tool and a commodity that could offer them financial security for the rest of their lives. They seem to know their value at a very early age; this is what is taught in rich girls' homes.

This story should give you an idea how wealth can become the main focus of one's life, where nothing else matters. While some low and middle class five-year-old girls are somewhere playing with their Barbie Dolls and learning how to finger paint. Here we have a wealthy-class five-year-old girl receiving lessons about her commodity from her mother. This is what was taught to her by her mother when she was just a child.

"Mommy!" little Taylor yelled out, trying to get her mother's attention.

"Yes, Taylor!" her mother yelled across the house as she sat in the living room getting a manicure from her personal manicurist, while her stylist brushed her hair.

"I need you, Mommy. I'm finished using the bathroom. I need you to clean me up."

"I will be there in a minute, Taylor."

"Okay, Mommy," said Taylor as she sat on the toilet waiting for her mother to come up stairs.

Taylor's mother, Megan, made her way to the upstairs bathroom to attend to her daughter.

"Let me first start off by showing you the proper way to wipe yourself after using the bathroom. I want you to take some tissue, roll it around your fingers until you feel that you have enough to clean yourself. When little girls wipe themselves, they wipe from the front to the back, never from the back to the front. You don't want to get boo boo on your little tu tu. Do you understand?"

"Yes, Mommy, I understand. Wipe from the front to the back and never from the back to the front."

"Good girl."

Ashley age thirteen, came upstairs to see what her mother and sister were doing. Taylor was excited to tell her big sister what her mother had taught her.

"So Ashley what do you know about your tu tu?"

"You mean my vagina, mom."

"Yes it's tu tu for Taylor and vagina for you."

"I know about sex mom if that's what you're referring to."

"No, I'm not talking about sex, per se; I want to talk to you about the importance of your vagina, your self worth, your commodity."

"I know what commodities are, Mom. Commodities are stuff like cotton, corn, sugar, and coffee."

"Good for you, and just like those things are commodities your vagina is just as valuable. Mom used her commodity to catch your dad. Mommy wants you to definitely keep away from broke guys, the women in our family are allergic to broke men. There's nothing they can do for any of us. As you grow up, the men you want to attract are rich, and wealthy regardless of their skin color."

"What's wrong with broke men, Mom. Some of my best male friends are broke?"

"You need to choose your boyfriends wisely, which is why I need you to keep those pretty legs of yours closed until Mr. Rich, and Wealthy comes along. You get out what you put in. This is your investment so take care of it. If you ever decide to give that little thing away, just remember that it's very valuable. This is your treasure and don't ever forget that, Ashley."

"I'm not going got argue with you, mom, however, I personally think it's wrong."

"My great, great, great, great grandmother was raised the same way, and I have no plans on changing the way I raise my daughters. You are a treasure, not some poor trailer trash or welfare recipient."

Unlike the other story about the poor girl, Simone and her mother, when both stories are compared, one mother felt that a trip to the 99 cent store was all she was worth. In this particular story, the mother teaches her teenage daughter about her commodity and her true worth. This is a story about how one thinks one way and another individual thinks another way.

They say that our lives are shaped by our thoughts, and I believe that. The importance of telling her daughter to wait until she's at least twenty years old before she starts to get serious with men was the right thing to do. The longer our young girls wait to have sex, the better off they turn out to be. Keeping sex off the brain and out of the mind is a good thing. If they participate in sexual intercourse, there's an eighty-five percent chance of them becoming pregnant. I feel it does a woman an injustice to herself when she goes from one man to another. Back in my day it was called "Bed Hopping." Every time you sleep with a different man, your commodity loses its value believe it or not. Following in the footsteps of other young girls that have no direction or purpose is never a good idea. Most young girls don't have a clue what they want out of life.

CNN News broadcasted a segment not long ago about girls as young as eleven that are already having sex, and it's becoming a normal thing for young girls to do in elementary school. Parents are not raising their daughters to avoid this. At eleven years old, you should be somewhere doing homework, reading a book, or maybe even learning how to cook a meal. Most young women today don't know how to fry an egg.

The true moral to this story is: Unless you think of yourself as a commodity, and that your worth goes beyond an outfit or a dinner at some cheap restaurant, you will continue to settle for less than you deserve.

The lesson in this story was not Megan's wealth it was the education that she instilled in her daughters at a young age. I do not believe that an individual has to be born into wealth in order to achieve wealth. Everything begins with a thought. If you grow up as a poor child, but you're always thinking about becoming rich, then maybe one day being rich is something you can achieve with education, wisdom, knowledge and drive.

Does a person have to be white? Absolutely not, the color of your skin does not give a person the ability to become rich, or wealthy, being rich or wealthy is a state of one's mind, first. The bank account is second.

In the above illustration, Megan never said that she had to become her husband's whore or freak. It also appears that her husband wanted something that many men did not have, and that was a woman that doesn't have many miles on her tires, which is why she became the chosen one. Having wealth starts in the mind and not the vagina, even though many believe it does. Believe it or not the vagina only gives an illusion to the imagination to men. This causes them to believe in their mind that they must have what they see, when in fact, they are choosing the entire woman and not only what's between her legs.

As I stated earlier, the majority of girls that are raised in low income housing or projects, usually don't get the same opportunities as those that were born with a silver spoon in their mouths.

Did Taylor and Ashley's mother show them how to become a high paid prostitute, absolutely not? She only felt it was her duty as a mother, to teach her daughters the value of their body. Was a price tag placed on these two girls bodies, absolutely not? In so many words she was telling her daughters that the man they date or decide to marry one day should be wealthy. In her mind I am sure what she was trying to tell Taylor and Ashley was. "If you're planning to have sex with a man, make the choice and have sex with one that can take care of you in the event you became pregnant. Know that you have become pregnant by someone that can take care of you and your child. Why settle with a poor man's penis when you can get the same type of penis with a whole lot more money attached to it."

Even though these two young ladies were taught to seek riches and wealth, it doesn't always turn out that way. I have witnessed rich and wealthy women date broke, low-down thugs in exchange for fun and excitement. That is something that most females don't get when they come from a rich and wealthy family. It has been revealed to me that broke, low-down thugs know how to party. They have swagger, one thing that most rich and wealthy men don't have.

Money isn't everything to some women even rich women. What good is it to have all the money in the world and sit around lonely and bored to death? This new generation believes in spending money and having a good time. Every day is like Christmas to them and every weekend is party time.

Do rich and wealthy women have it going on? Of course they do, as far as money is concerned. However, do they have it going on between their legs? This is not always true and I only say this because of experience and true knowledge. Money, riches, wealth or a mansion plays no part when it comes to the vagina. The V is in a whole other category and stands alone from everything else.

Chapter Eleven

Surrender to the V

Surrendering to the vagina has always been a problem for some men. A majority of men tend to believe that it's the man that holds the power, and the man controls everything. In some cases, women feel like second class citizens. Why shouldn't they? A woman's income is at least 20% less than what a man makes doing the same job, or holding the same position. It wasn't long ago when women had to fight to be able to vote or to have their voices heard in this country. Many years ago, men felt as though the woman's job was in the kitchen; pleasing him in the bedroom; and raising the kids. In those days it was the woman who surrendered to the man.

As we all know, today we live in a different country, a country where there are equal rights for all. Where women's voices are being heard, and their messages are been understood by men, politicians, and the rest of society.

Men need to bow down and surrender to the vagina because the woman knows that a man cannot live on water, bread, and money alone. It's the woman's vagina that brings life into this world. It's the woman's vagina that brings joy and pain to a man. Of course, pain only comes into play when the woman decides to take her vagina somewhere else, or surrender herself to someone else.

To all men, let's surrender ourselves to the vagina and give respect to every female on earth. Let's start admiring our women for being the amazing beings they are. Let's thank our women for being our backbone. Let's thank our women for being our supporters. Let's thank women for being our comfort zone. Let's give honor to all the mothers in the world that endure the morning sickness and pain they went through while giving birth to us. Let's just surrender to the vagina.

Chapter Twelve

Sharing of the V

I speak for every man that has ever experienced the joy and pain that comes from being with a woman. We thank you for sharing the vagina with us, which brought us so much joy. I would like to share with you the first time a vagina was shared with me.

I was only twelve years old and the girl who shared it with me was twelve also. One early Saturday morning, my two brothers, my five sisters, and I went looking for bottles in trash cans and dumpsters. I remembered us making a total of fifty cents each that day. Usually, we gave the money to our mother to help pay the bills or to buy food, but on this particular Saturday, she told us we could keep the money to buy candy. I decided that I would only spend half my money on candy and save the rest for something I wanted.

Later that evening, I went downstairs to apartment number 1, and asked to speak with Arlean. Arlean's older brother Kevin, came to the door, and looked at me as if I had done something to him. He asked, "What do you want with my sister, Arlean?"

I replied, "I want to talk to her."

He came closer to me and said, "My sister can't talk or hear she is deaf."

Since there was something that I wanted from her, I asked him, "Can she come out to play?"

He went to go get her and I stood there sweating. After a minute or two, she came outside with a pencil and tablet; she sat on the ground, and began to write a note.

"Hi, Johnny Boy, How are you?"

"I sat down next to her to read the note, and then she handed me the pencil and tablet for me to respond back to her.

So I wrote. "Hi, Arlean, I'm doing okay."

I handed the tablet back to her, and she began writing again. "What made you come downstairs to talk to me, and what do you want?"

I wrote back. "I came down to talk to you because I like you, and what I want is . . ." Then I stopped writing for a minute because I became shy and a little afraid, because what I wanted was the same thing she had been giving all the other little boys in the neighborhood. She looked at me with a smile and began to lick her lips. I grabbed the pencil tight to finish writing. "I have a quarter for some coochie. Can I have some?" She snatched the tablet from me and wrote me a quick note, and handed it back to me.

The note read, "Give me the money, and meet me in the garage."

I jumped up, handed her two dimes and a nickel, and ran to the garage to wait for her. Now, this is my first time ever doing anything like this, but I had heard the other little boys talk about coochie, and how good it made them feel, and I wanted to feel good like them. While waiting in the dark old garage I became nervous because I didn't know the first thing about sex. I heard the door open slowly, it was Arlean, and she took off her clothes, and lay down on the ground. She began waving her hands, as if she was saying, "Come on, come to me." I laid down on top of her with my clothes on, she unzipped my pants, took out my little penis, and tried to put it inside her. She took full control, and five minutes later, we left.

I ran upstairs and grabbed my math book to do my homework. As I sat there, I realized it didn't make me feel good, and I wanted my money back! While sitting there thinking about what happened to me, I thought about what I could have bought with my quarter and said to myself, "I'll never give another girl any money for sex!" I fell asleep with my head in my math book that night.

Of course, I was just a kid when I felt that way. Since that first episode with Arlean back in 1971, I have had my share of vaginas in my lifetime, and of course, my attitude toward vaginas is much different today. I have had vaginas that brought me joy and excitement, and I have had a few vaginas that I wish I could erase from my memory bank. As I got older, I found out that when a woman shares her vagina with a man it becomes pleasing, and it can become addicting to some men, which is how most females end up finding out about their power. Women share their vagina with men, and men end up enjoying their power, and when they say jump, we ask how high. It's no different with a drug addiction; the drug in this case is the *power force*. It can cause an individual to become unable to function like a normal person in society. A man can develop an unbearable mood swing towards everyone he meets. It becomes difficult for him to sleep at night, and he may find himself walking the streets looking for more drugs.

This is one of the reasons why we men seek to find a way to earn a decent living, or turn to illegal activities. Then once we get the money, we want we go out and purchase nice cars and SUV's along with nice clothes, jewelry, furs and mink coats, homes, and mansions. It is what brings us out to night clubs and other social gatherings. We're looking for the next vagina that would consider sharing themselves if only for one night.

I have come to realize that it's the woman's choice who she decides to share her power with, and not the man, which means, the power lies in the hands of the woman. We're just hoping to get laid for a night, or for a lifetime.

A message from me to all the women in the world is, "Keep on sharing that vagina with us men, making this world a wonderful place to live in."

Chapter Thirteen

Good V vs. Bad V

There's no such thing as a good vagina or a bad vagina. It's all in the mind of the man. Each man feels a certain way when it comes down to the vagina he's engaged in at that moment and time. Of course, there are some women who would like to think, and believe that they have the best vagina in the whole wide world, and no other vagina on the planet can do what theirs can do. Okay! I must admit. There are some women who have taken the time to develop their skills. I give you ladies that have developed your skills, your due respect. Then, you have some women out there who spend a lot of time manicuring themselves in order to attract a certain type of men. I take my hat off to you as well, but at the end of the day. It's still just a vagina.

What makes a woman's vagina good to a man may vary according to the chemistry in the relationship.

Now when it comes to the bad vaginas, it simply means that the two individuals do not meet each other's specifications.

Even though it's all in the mind of a man, to determine what's good or bad, there are still some things that must be performed in order for a man to pass judgment.

In today's society, the word "bad" represents "good." So one must know when a man is saying bad to mean bad, or bad to mean good.

The old saying "a woman that has large breasts and a nice-sized behind represents a good vagina," this is only a myth in society. Good isn't based on large breasts or a nice-sized behind. Again! It goes back to what I said earlier. It's all in the mind of the man. The average man identifies large breasts and a big behind to be something that can offer him the best temporary pleasure. Does it mean she has good vagina? No! Does it mean she has bad vagina? No! It only means she has large breasts and a nice big behind that comes along with her vagina.

Instead of taking my definition of the words "good" and "bad," let's see what *Webster's Dictionary* says:

"Good" means producing favorable results; honorable: worthy: as one's good name, enjoyable, agreeable, happy, etc. dependable: reliable: right: adequate: ample; sufficient; satisfying; as a good meal, well behaved; dutiful; able; skilled; expert; worth; virtue; merit; an exclamation of satisfaction, and pleasure."

"Bad" means not good; not as it should be; defective in quality; below standard; lacking in worth; inadequate; unskilled; unfavorable; unpleasant; rotted; decomposed; spoiled; faulty."

Again! This is all in the mind of a man, unless the woman they lie down with falls in the description of the word "bad."

Most men associate an attractive female with having a good vagina, while others see an unattractive female as having a bad vagina. I have yet to see a vagina on the face of a woman. For those who don't know where it's located, the vagina is between the females two legs and around six to twelve inches below her navel. A pretty or unattractive face has nothing to do with whether the vagina is good or bad. Some men think that a pretty-faced woman makes her more tolerable to look at while making love or having sex. But it has been reported by millions of men across the world that unattractive women have some of the best vagina in the world. They say the uglier the woman is, the better the sex is because she knows deep inside she must perform her best so that she can have a repeat interlude with the same man. It's like having a gun and one bullet. You have one shot to hit your target.

It has also been reported that many pretty-faced women tend to be less aggressive in their lovemaking. They lie there in bed with the notion that the man should do all the work in bed while they sit there looking pretty, which is why in many cases, the fine and beautiful women end up losing their man to a woman who's less attractive.

There are also rumors that an unattractive woman has a bad-smelling vagina and they neglect their female responsibilities. They refuse to visit a gynecologist every six months or fail to take an STD test to monitor themselves internally. They tend to get the bad rap on the streets unlike the attractive woman with the pretty face, money, or fame who have some of the same habits.

Who really determines who has a good vagina or a bad vagina? Several questions come to mind like; Is it the person who's receiving it? Or is it the one who's giving it away? Is it the woman with the unattractive face and beautiful body, or is it the woman with the pretty face and no body? Is it the woman with alot of money? Or is it the woman that's on welfare with eight kids? Is it the woman that we see on television or on movie screens, or is it the woman that' isn't known to the world? The next time we decide to pay a woman a compliment regarding her vagina, decide who deserves the compliment.

Chapter Fourteen

Old V Is Like Fine Wine

Some say old vagina is like fine wine. It just gets better with time. Since I am not a woman, I wouldn't know that, so I spoke to a group of women over forty to get their opinion and answers to the question, if they felt that the V is really like wine as it matures. Not being a wine drinker, I wouldn't know the difference between a bottle of six-day-old wine and a bottle of sixty-year-old wine. However, I have heard that wine does get better as it ages.

You might say to yourself, "Why does this matter, it has nothing to do with power?" I would have to agree, but I believe that a compliment should be given to a woman every chance we get the opportunity to give one, and if the statement is true that old V's are like fine wine, then my compliment goes out to those women.

One Saturday evening I was invited to a women's social meeting that was held at the president of the social group's meeting place. I had the opportunity to ask all of them the same question, and their responses were surprisingly varied. But, they were all willing to answer my questions without hesitation. First I addressed the question to a woman named Ruby. Ruby said she was fifty years old, and looked as good as a glass of red wine if I had to say so myself.

"So Ruby, Do you believe that old vagina is much better than young vagina?"

She replied, "For starters, I was young myself, and I can truly say that what I thought I knew back then, didn't compare to what I know today. Things like keeping ourselves in shape, learning new moves in the bedroom, and knowing how to use those moves when it's time to," said Ruby.

"Would you say that older vagina is like fine wine?"

"Of course," said Ruby

We all laughed.

"Seriously, there are tricks that older women can do that young girls haven't mastered yet," Ruby answered.

"Would you like to share some of those tricks?"

"As they say in the streets, 'the game is to be sold, not to be told.' If I tell you my tricks, the whole female population would know, and that, my friend, would make it even more difficult for women like me to get younger men in the sack," Ruby answered with a grin on her face.

"Let's get back to the original question, then. Are you ladies aware that there will be millions of young women reading this novel saying to themselves that 'an old woman has got nothing on us younger women?' What would you say to those young women that think, and feel that way?"

"At age fifty, I have the experience, for one, and there are things that a younger woman just doesn't know. First of all, younger women today take sex for granted. They get high or take an ecstasy pill and screw every Tom, Dick, and Harry in the club. Half of them don't even wash their behind after they are finished having sex, and most of them don't know how to please a man. At least a real man," Ruby answered.

"What's the difference between a man and real man?" I asked.

"A man doesn't give a damn about making love when they lay down with a woman all they want to do is satisfy themselves. A real man appreciates good sex as art. You just don't hop on top of a woman for a few minutes and call it a day. It's like you're painting a Picasso. You need to take your time," Ruby answered.

The next person I spoke to was Betty. Betty was sixty-one years old and appeared to be in great shape. She had on a pair of Seven Jeans and a pink sleeveless T-shirt.

"So Betty, do you believe that old vagina is much better than young vagina?"

"I'm sure you've heard the phrase 'It gets better with time,' haven't you?"

"I have."

"An old vagina is like an old antique automobile. The older the car, the more that car is worth. It's the same with the vagina. The older we women get, the less we use it, which automatically makes it become priceless. We're gentler, we move much slower than the younger females. We have learned many things in the bedroom over the years, things that smart women never share," said Betty.

"These young women today want everything right now. Their relationships are like fast-food restaurants, drive in, and drive out," Betty exclaimed.

"Would you say that older vagina is like fine wine?"

"I can't speak for every other older woman, but I can speak for myself. I have the secret."

"Maybe another time you'll tell me what that is," I said.

Betty laughed. "Yes, maybe I will."

"Ok, thank you." Now I would like to ask Stephanie, Carol, and Paula, "Do you believe that old vagina is much better than young vagina?"

"Should I go first?" Stephanie asked the other two ladies

"Sure!" Paula answered.

"My first experience with a man was twenty years ago, and I am seventy-one now so, I was a late bloomer."

"So you're seventy-one years of age?" I asked.

"That is correct, and I feel as if I am forty. I don't just let anyone drive into my garage; I pick and choose my partner."

"So you agree that older vagina is like fine wine?"

"Yes, because it has aged gracefully and it's vintage"

"It's your turn Carol." I said.

"For me, I would like to believe it is. I'm very picky about who I share my body with. The absence of casual sexual intercourse gives me bragging rights to compare myself to a bottle of fine wine. You don't drive a Rolls Royce every day, do you?" Carol asked me.

"You are absolutely right."

"If you did own one, would you drive it all over town?" Carol asked once again.

"No, I wouldn't."

"That's my point. Everything worth something isn't misused or abused. I believe when a woman reaches a certain age, especially over the age of fifty, her vagina becomes her pride and joy. The hopping and bumping, having your salad tossed and the grinding all stops. Oh, and as far as slapping it and rubbing it around, that too comes to a stop," said Carol.

"Okay! Paula, do you want to answer the question I asked the other two ladies?"

"My vagina looks better than a nineteen-year-old girl's, and I make sure of that. I have my vagina surgically lifted every six months," Paula answered.

"Like Carol said, every woman over the age forty-five has a secret why they think old vagina is like fine wine," Paula answered.

"Do you believe that old vagina is much better than young vagina?" I asked Ella.

"Well I am a virgin and so I don't think I'm qualified to answer that question," said Ella.

"How old are you, if you don't mind me asking?"

"I don't mind. I'm seventy-seven," Ella answered.

"If I didn't know any better, I would have guessed that you were in your late forties."

"Come now! Don't you think you're stretching it just a bit much?" Ella asked.

Ella crossed her legs and picked up her coffee cup to take a sip.

"I think that old vagina is like fine wine, I know it to be true because, the best wine is made of the finest grapes in the country," concluded Ella.

The above stories were enlightening for me. What I learned is that once most women reach the age of forty, some of them give themselves a reality check. Most women become aware that it's time for a mental and physical evaluation. Their diet changes, exercising becomes important, they get plenty of rest, and they become more conscious of the things that are important to them.

These women are an example of class, wisdom and style. Being healthy and staying in shape was another thing that I noticed about these ladies. Surprisingly, I didn't see one tattoo on any of their bodies. They expressed and demonstrated how women should feel good about themselves. Women should realize who they are, by finding their own individuality, and not trying to identify themselves through someone else, or through material possessions.

Over the past five years I have heard women say things like, "Life doesn't start until a woman reaches age forty," and "Life after forty is when some women began to really look at themselves from the inside out and reevaluate their lives more often.

I see nothing wrong with an older or mature woman trying to make her mark in life when she's out in public, as long as she does it with class and style. Teenagers and young adult females should pattern themselves after ladies with a positive self esteem. They should pattern themselves after ladies who have morals and values such as the ones from the social club. If they were taught how to conduct themselves at an early age, there is no doubt in my mind, that our young ladies and our soon to be young ladies would be respected by all males. Men will respect you instead of looking at you as though you are some street whore or a hood rat. Respect starts with you, and respect is worn on the outside, but it is embedded from within. It is also shown in your body movements and your actions.

To the young women who are under the age of forty, get ready to go through a change in your life that will take you to another dimension. It's about aging gracefully, and there is nothing wrong with growing older, because a mature woman is truly as good as a bottle of the finest wine.

Chapter Fifteen

The Lost V

The word "lost" *means not to be found; missing; parted with; no longer seen, heard from, or known; a person lost in the crowd; not gained or won; attended with defeat; having wandered from the way; bewildered; perplexed; usefully wasted.* The increase in teenage pregnancy in America alone is a clear indication that the vagina is lost. There are young girls all over the world who become engaged in sexual intercourse at ages that are entirely too young.

Not long ago, I heard one of the news stations report that young girls are starting to engage in sexual intercourse at age nine. At nine years old, you don't know anything about sex; you barely know the proper way to sit in a skirt.

The vagina has truly become lost in today's society, and most young girls have no idea that their vagina is lost.

When most teenage girls run away, they end up on the streets looking for a place to stay. Many of them don't know it, but they are actually looking for a place for their vagina to stay, because if they find a home, and the home belongs to a man, more than likely he's taking them in his home because of the vagina, and only the vagina. Why do men roam the streets looking for teenage girls to offer them temporary shelter, and food to eat at no cost? They do this because young girls have something to offer, the vagina comes with the package.

Young girls today know how important it is for them to keep themselves looking good while seeking love. Many of them don't have a high school diploma or a GED. Most of the time they come from broken homes where there is no male figure in the household. The majority of single mothers spend all their time working for minimum wage just to keep a roof over their heads, and food on the table. This leaves many teenage girls free to walk the streets.

A lost vagina is all it is, nothing more nothing less. If parents teach their young daughters the importance of remaining a virgin until marriage, they would have a much better life. Then young teenage girls could grow up, and maybe go to college, instead of being a lost soul looking for love in all the wrong places.

Not knowing one's worth or value can cause any female to feel unwanted and lost. If most of the young, and let's not exclude many older females, had some direction in their lives, there would be no such thing as a lost vagina in the world. Sometimes that loss can cause a person to give up on life. We all know that if a woman didn't have a vagina, there would be no love to find.

When does a female know when she's lost?

You can tell by her sexual activities. When a vagina finds a home and a man is in the home, there will be plenty of intimacy in their home. The female is usually happier when her vagina is not lost.

A lost vagina needs to be loved, even if the female doesn't have anyone to love them. Every so often, the vagina could remind the female that it's time to "feed the cat" in so many words.

A vagina also remains lost and single when it's attached to a female that finds something wrong with every man she meets. No one is good enough to have her love, or to make love to them, which ends up leaving the lost vagina alone and lonely. It's the female that decides how long she will allow her vagina to remain lost. They make all the decisions when it comes to allowing a man to have sexual intercourse with them. In order for a female to know whether their vagina is lost, or has been found, they must first know the definition of the word "lost." In my opinion there is a word that every female should know. Learn what the word "lost" means and offer your vagina as an option, an option to remain lost or an option to be found by someone who's willing to offer a home to the vagina and you.

Chapter Sixteen

The Home Wrecker V

At the request of friends and acquaintances of both sexes who felt as though I should take the time to write a chapter about women who deliberately single out, and date *only* married men, here it is.

As I gathered my thoughts I could only think back to 1998. I actually knew a young woman that fit this particular category of women. People in the neighborhood called her a "Home Wrecker," because she didn't care about the marriages or the families she destroyed. This is a story about a young woman whose name is Karen.

It was a beautiful sunny Saturday afternoon, and Karen was sitting on the steps of an apartment complex where she lived. She was listening to some music when an older woman named Debra Wilcox was walking home from the grocery store. After having words with Karen, Mrs. Wilcox went home to put her groceries away. Approximately one hour later she returns to pay Karen a special visit. After Mrs. Wilcox's visit, Karen was rushed to the hospital and had to undergo emergency surgery. Mrs. Wilcox was arrested and released on bail, and it was months before Karen was able to return home. Let me take you back to that Saturday afternoon.

"Hi Mrs. Wilcox," Karen said as Mrs. Wilcox walked up to her.

Mrs. Wilcox stopped, sat her bags down and gave Karen a piece of her mind.

"How dare you speak to me you nasty heifer? When you were nothing but a nappy-headed little ole girl running up and down the street, I would let you come into my home to eat with my family because I felt sorry for you. I treated you as if you were one of my own. Don't you sit your behind there and speak to me after sleeping with my husband. You ain't nothing but a low-down dirty tramp."

"Mrs. Wilcox, it was your husband who approached me. Not once did I try to get with him, and now you are all up in my face calling me out of my name because you couldn't keep your husband's penis at home," Karen said as she sat their bopping her head to the music.

"If I was fifteen years younger, I would beat the living-shit out of you, and then spit on you when I was finished."

"That's not a way to speak to a lady, now, is it, Mrs. Wilcox."

"If I saw a lady I would respect her. You go to hell." Mrs. Wilcox says.

"Can I take your sweet, kind husband with me?" Karen asks as she laughs, and continues to bob her head to the music.

Mrs. Wilcox stared at Karen with the sign of death in her eyes. Seconds later another woman walked up and joined Mrs. Wilcox, she was in her late forties; her name was Judy.

"Is everything all right Mrs. Wilcox?" Judy asked.

"My day was fine until I ran into the devil," She answered.

"You must be Judy from down the street," Karen said.

"How do you know my name, and who are you?" Judy asked Karen.

"You don't know me, but I know your husband, Jack. Jack and I are friends."

Mrs. Wilcox turned and looked over at Judy and said; "Does this tramp know your husband?"

"I have no idea. This is my first time ever seeing this woman in my life," Judy answered.

"If she knows your husband, be careful," Mrs. Wilcox replied.

"What do I need to be careful about?"

"This woman has slept with my husband and at least six other women's husbands around here."

"Okay, but what does that have to do with my Jack. Jack is a faithful and honest man," Judy replied.

"That is what they all think." Karen said under her breath.

"What did you say?" Judy asks Karen."

"Just talking to myself."

"Mrs. Wilcox, I'm on my way home. Do you need any help with your bags?" Judy asks.

"I suppose I can use a little help, it's good to know that there are still some good honest women in this world," Mrs. Wilcox said as she hands Judy one of her bags and headed home.

An hour later, Karen is still listening to her music, her eyes are closed her mind and her body is engaged in the music. She did not see or hear Mrs. Wilcox approach her with a pot of scolding hot baby oil.

"You take this bitch," Says Mrs. Wilcox, and she threw the oil in Karen's face.

Karen jumped up screaming, runs in the house, and her mother dialed 9-1-1.

Mrs. Wilcox walked home with her head up, swinging the empty pot mumbling, "That will teach that bitch. I bet her ass will think twice before she messes with another woman's husband."

Three months later, Karen comes home from the hospital with bandages covering almost her entire face. She is sitting on the porch, reading her bible.

Minutes later, Dee Dee, who is one of Karen's friends, pulls up in brand new Camaro.

"Hey girl, what are you doing sitting out here on the steps and you just got out of the hospital? Shouldn't you be in bed resting?"

"No, said Karen, I needed some fresh air. I'm just sitting here reading my bible."

"I wanted to stop by and check on you. I am getting ready to meet Larry for dinner."

"Which Larry; Betty's husband, Larry, Karen asked?"

"Yeah, why?"

"Why? Look at me Dee Dee. What happened to me is the result of me messing with somebody else's' husband."

"Her husband came on to me a few months ago, and now I got him sprung. He told me that he wasn't happy with his wife, and he told me that he didn't love her anymore. In six months he's going to divorce her and move in with me. Within a year I could become Mrs. Walker."

"Why are you doing this?"

"Because his wife has something that I want, and look who's talking? You were 'Ms. Home Wrecker,' in the flesh. You destroyed at least 5 families that I know of, and you are indirectly responsible for causing one of those wives to be admitted to the mental ward."

Karen did not respond to Dee Dee's comment.

Seconds later Pam, another one of Karen's friend pulled up in a brand new BMW. She gets out of the car, walks to the porch and sat down on the other side of Karen. She hugged her and said, "I heard what happened, girl. I am so sorry that happened to you."

Dee Dee asked Pam. "Are you still dating the guy that owns the construction company?"

"Yes, I am still dating him," answered Pam.

Karen then said to both of them, "You guys need to stop playing games with these married men. I'm done with that!"

"GAMES!" Dee Dee shouted.

"Games? Look who's talking," Pam points her finger at Karen. "You dated married men for fun." Pam points her finger at Dee Dee and says, "You date married men looking for a husband by trying to take someone else's husband, which is stupid to me. Now on the other hand, I date married men strictly for what they can do for me. I figure if I'm going to lower my moral standards and play second position to another woman, it has to be worth my while," Pam said without taking a breath.

Dee Dee gets up and said to Pam, "you have some nerve calling me stupid because I am dating married men to find a husband; you date married men so they can buy you clothes and a car, now that's stupid? I'm out of here, talk to you later, Karen." She stoops down to give Karen a hug.

Pam says, "I just came by to check on you. I have somewhere I have to be. I will talk to you later. Glad you are home you got my number call me if you need me."

As Pam and Dee Dee prepare to leave, Karen says to both of them. "You are both stupid. Remember: Karma is a bitch and it can come back and bite you in the ass. Look at me. You should really consider what you are doing; carefully think about it, and picture me looking like this. This could happen to one of you. Love you guys. Talk to you later."

They both gave her a hug and left.

The above Illustration is just one of many scenarios how women, mainly single women, prey on married men. They do not care, nor do they consider the families, and the lives that they are destroying, because they are heartless and inconsiderate. They usually suffer from low self-esteem, with no morals or self-respect. Most women that engage in a relationship with a married man are not ready for a full-time relationship. This type of woman enjoys the flexibility of having a man for her needs, but not having a man around all the time. It's like baby-sitting your sister's kids. At any given time you can give those kids back. The down side to all this is, if that man passes away, the life insurance, home, bank accounts, 401K's, social security benefits, and everything else goes to the WIFE. The mistress doesn't receive anything, so the time she spent with him was time wasted at the end of the day. Some people say that women who stoop that low to date someone else's husband have no respect for another woman.

What many women are doing today is settling for second position, and in some cases third, fourth or tenth position, and they don't even know it. In my opinion these women are self-centered, and selfish they don't care about who they are hurting, or the pain that they inflict on the families. These women become the predator, married men become the prey, and wives become the unwilling victims. What these predators don't realize is that they become the man's private, on-call, paid hooker.

It seems as though single women dating married men is becoming an epidemic. The majority of married men offer financial assistance to these women, especially because the mistress knows that the man is married.

I believe if a man is married, he should act like he is married. In the event he is not happy, it makes no sense to remain in a marriage where the wife is the only one married in the relationship. Instead of cheating or being miserable, legally end your marriage, and allow your wife the opportunity to find happiness elsewhere. Instead of taking money out of your household, bank accounts, credit cards, or the kids college fund to give to another woman outside of your marriage why not go on a second honeymoon? You should make an attempt to repair your marriage with the one you once loved before looking for another woman.

Husbands, you must stop misleading other women into believing that you are not happy in your marriage, that you are getting a divorce, that you are separated from your wife or that you haven't had sex with your wife in a while. Leave your wedding ring on your finger; stop taking it off when you go out to bars, nightclubs and grocery stores. Try spending more time with your wife, express what you have on your mind relating to your marriage. Give her the chance to fulfill the wants and desires that you may have. Remember, when you took your vows there was only you, your wife to be, and the minister at the altar. Not a mistress.

And wives don't nag your husband's all the time. Try being supportive, and pay attention to his needs, wants, and desires. Don't ignore his body language and his silence. These are usually signs that your husband is preparing to cheat. This is the time that you should sit down with him and be the partner you were chosen to be. I believe a little conversation and romance can repair anything. You don't have to become a victim of a home wrecker. Remember that romance doesn't always mean sex either.

Chapter Seventeen

Silver, Gold & Platinum V Diggers

For years, people have been under the impression that there is only one type of "Digger," and that is a "Gold Digger." When in fact, there are actually three types of diggers. The first digger is the "Silver Digger." This type of digger will offer themselves to any man regardless of his financial status; he could be riding public transportation, on a skateboard, walking, homeless, on welfare, and even on drugs. He can buy her a cheap swap meet outfit, a pair of Payless shoes or burger and fries without the drink, and that would be just fine with her. Silver Diggers will accept credit, for example; a man tells her that he is going to give her ten dollars, but he gives her five dollars, and then tells her he will owe her the other five dollars the next month. Some people might call silver diggers "Hood Rats." It doesn't take much to get a Silver Digger.

Many of us in society will confuse a woman that is seeking financial security with a man before settling down with him as a "Digger," but in fact, these women are only seeking security for what might become their future. I can understand why a woman does not want to be with someone that is a "nobody," particularly if she is already financially independent, but how does a man know if he is in the presence of a "Digger?" She usually does not identify herself as one, and there is seldom an emotional connection between a digger and a man. Diggers usually have only one thing on their mind, and that is to find a way to dig into her man's pocket, bank account and eventually his pension plan.

Diggers comes in all ages, shapes, sizes and colors. They are not usually liked by many women; and they are hated by many weak men, men that usually get taken advantage of by manipulative women.

Don't get mad or hate a Silver, Gold or Platinum Digger. These women have different motives, and an unusual way of getting men to buy them things, and to pay their bills. Anyone can become a "Digger."

The second type of Digger is the "Gold Digger." These particular types of women look for men that drive the Range Rovers, Bentleys, Mercedes Benz, or any other high-end car. This type of woman hangs out at nightclubs, and is usually in the V.I.P. section. As long as he's got money flowing, he can be a baller, drug dealer, or bank robber, it really doesn't matter. They are more concerned with his outer image, his car, his clothes, and his home.

The second group of Gold Diggers goes after working class and military men with benefits. The majority of these women camp out, or re-locate their residence near Army, Navy or Marine bases. Their plan is to capture themselves a man from the armed forces, settle down, have one or two children, and live off their man's benefits. In order for these gold diggers to catch such a man they hang out in night clubs not far from the base. They offer themselves to any man, regardless of his race, religion, skin color, weight, height, disabilities, or looks.

Let's not discount these Gold Diggers. They have studied their victims well. These women are familiar with each and every one of the military ranks and salaries. An E-5 and E-6 ranking man is usually captured by women in their 20's or early 30's. The women over thirty-five concentrate on men with a ranking of E-7 and above. These ranks come with a lifetime health plan and other financial commodities.

A man with an E-7 or higher rank could receive unemployment pay, hazard pay, separation pay, and other "extra" payments. The plus side to these higher level ranks is that their monies are non-taxable.

The Gold Digger does not discriminate, even if he is an alcoholic or drug addict, as long as he receives a check with benefits to support her mission. They will use their vagina to capture and marry their prey, which in some cases allows them to file for citizenship and be brought back to America.

Then there is the "Platinum Gold Digger." These women are in a class of their own. There is no other woman in the world that can compare to them. Unlike the Silver and Gold Digger who tell their business to other low, and mid-budget women, the Platinum Gold Diggers never kiss and tell.

These women typically have no feelings and share no emotions when it comes to a man, which is why they are able to play the game so well. By the time these women reach the age of thirty-five they are usually "heartless."

There are also those that have retired from the game, and as a retired Platinum Digger, they sometimes run into a younger woman who has the potential of becoming a Platinum Digger, so they invest the time to teach and train them how to become a professional Platinum Digger. It's like an old dog teaching the young "pup" new tricks.

There is a huge difference between a Platinum Digger, and a Gold Digger. The Platinum Digger is usually up-front with men, as opposed to the Gold Digger who will just blend in with the crowd, picking up the crumbs left by a Platinum Digger.

Platinum Diggers are not hookers, or prostitutes. They have no plans to rent or lease themselves for an hour or a month. They compare themselves to an American Express Black card, "Priceless." These women are not cheap. Their fees are usually half a million dollar homes or condos, one hundred and seventy nine thousand dollar Bentleys,' GT Convertibles, fifty thousand dollar Piaget watches, hundred thousand dollar VS1 F-color stones with GIA Certificate documentation. They are given unlimited Platinum credit cards, several personal bank accounts in their name, 401k's, million dollar life insurance policies, ten thousand dollar a week allowances, and expensive hair weaves. High Budget equals high maintenance.

Platinum Diggers look for status, and wealth. You can be a regular Bill Doe, or Bill Gates. As long as your money flows as long as the Interstate 5, you have action at pulling a Platinum Digger. This type of woman cannot be found in the hood, night clubs, malls, sport bars, strip bars, Venice Beach, movies, or bus stops. These women are usually spotted at political banquets or fundraisers, where dinners are typically twenty-five hundred dollars a plate. They shop on Rodeo Drive with their Pomeranian dog, in their oversize Channel handbags. They pull up in valet, and step out of their sport cars; they dine at places like Mr. Chows or Mastro. They go to Broadway plays in NYC or major art galleries; they frequent Newport Beach to lie in the white sand while getting a tan.

Platinum Diggers know their designers like Salvatore Ferragamo, Gucci, Christian Dior, and Channel, just to name a few.

While other Gold Diggers look for working class and military men, the Platinum Digger concentrates on actors earning ten million plus per year, athletes earning five million a year or business men that are CEO's of fortune 500 corporations earning ten million plus per year with bonuses. These women know what they want and they know where to find it.

I actually met a Platinum Digger while visiting the Getty Museum in Bel Air, California. It was a Saturday afternoon around 2:30pm, when I noticed a tall dark skinned woman with long hair that lay across her shoulders. She was wearing a Prada dress, a pair of Prada three inch high heels. She had a Prada handbag in one hand, and an art gallery booklet in the other. She stood there admiring a painting through her dark Christian Dior shades. She looked to be in her late thirties or early forties. I decided to slowly walk over and stand beside her, and make small talk, as she stared at the expensive painting.

I said, "If you like it, I'll buy it."

The woman slowly looked to her right, and noticed me standing beside her. She then leaned back, and looked at me from head to toe before responding to what she felt was a silly comment.

"If I wanted it, I could buy it myself, unlike some people who are just looking for conversation. Besides, this is a Picasso. It's worth between fifteen and twenty million dollars. If I want it, I can buy it. Can you afford to buy it?"

"No."

"You are way out of your league. Maybe you should find yourself a Silver or Gold Digger. Your money isn't long enough for me. My monthly expenses are close to a hundred thousand."

"I was merely making small talk with you since it appears that you and I are the only African Americans in this art museum."

"You see, there is nothing you can buy me that I can't buy myself, so unless you're Will Smith, making twenty million a movie, or Donald Trump the Billionaire, you may want to consider flirting with the young lady that's working behind the concession stand. The one that's serving people slices of pizza and Coke."

"You got jokes."

"Jokes do not interest me, and I would like to stand here alone and admire this painting, if you don't mind."

As I walked off, she mumbled beneath her breath "Broke men have nothing to offer but silly jokes, and lame conversation."

Whether a digger is silver, gold or platinum, they are all the same. They are no different than a prostitute. A prostitute charges a certain amount of money for services; a digger never tells you that you are being charged. They take until you stop giving.

What makes a woman find a career in "Gold Digging?" I believe at some point she probably said something to herself like, "I'm tired of sleeping around for nothing in exchange. I need to get something out of the deal." A Digger isn't like every other woman. Most of them don't believe in working a nine-to-five. They believe that everything should come to them easily, without any hard work ever being done. Some of them feel that they can talk their way into a man's pocket, while others feel they can lay on their back to get what they feel they have coming to them. Diggers look for a man that has something to offer, even if it's a cheap meal from a fast food restaurant. When it's free, the digger feels as though she has accomplished something, when in fact, what they receive could very well come from a man that simply likes them and nothing more.

Chapter Eighteen

The V Recession

While people sit around trying to decide if the world is really in a recession, many women are finding themselves working two jobs, raising children, being a housewife, and maintaining a healthy relationship. They are finding themselves, and their vagina, falling into a recession. Men still want to have sex, and women are finding themselves not in the mood for sex, intimacy, or some man jumping up and down inside of them. In some cases, when there's no money being brought into the home both the vagina, and the woman shut down. She is not in the mood, and the vagina finds a place to rest until her partner, the woman, mentally and emotionally feels up to having sex, or making love. This does not place money over the vagina. However, most women function better when the bills are paid every month; when food is on the table and gas is in the car.

Some women find themselves headed towards vagina recession when they become depressed, or when they are under tremendous emotional stress. Stress usually affects the performance of a woman while she's having sex, or when making love to her partner. I can recall the day when a female friend of mine went into a vagina depression. She and I used to have sex from time to time, when neither one of us was in a serious relationship. When she went into depression mode, it was over for us sexually. She didn't want me to touch her at all. I used to tease her and she would say something like, "My vagina is so damn depressed, the both of us are in a recession." That was the first time anyone explained it that way to me.

I could understand a woman not wanting to have sex while on her period, or due to some illness, but a vagina being in a recession was a new one for me. Of course, I accepted what she said because she was my friend, and when you are friends, it is not about the vagina or the penis. It is about being there for that person you call a friend.

This goes out to the men in the world. The next time your wife, woman, girlfriend, lady, lover, or boo tells you that she's not feeling well, remember this chapter, "The Vagina Recession." Your woman's vagina could be in a vagina recession. So give her some space. Let her, and her vagina have their recession time to themselves. Be there to comfort them during this difficult time they are going through. Show them your support. Be that friend she needs, and let her know that you love her regardless of, or despite, what she's going through. This is my advice to men in the world, try and remember the country is not the only thing that is dealing with a recession. Sometimes your significant other is too.

Chapter Nineteen

V Obsession

While the murder rate in the nation has increased from gang violence to robberies, so has the rate of rape and murders of women.

For years, sick-minded men have gone out to hunt for their prey. They not only rape their victims, but they often murder them. The vagina has caused men to force themselves on women because they have to have it, or they want to prove that they are in control. There have even been many cases reported where men have raped and murdered young girls under the age of six.

How does the vagina carry so much power that is causes one to take, steal, and even kill for it? This has been a question I have asked myself for many years.

There are reports of husbands that murder their own wives because she simply attempted to divorce him. I believe it is a weak man who reaches a point in his life where he contemplates taking another human being's life over something that doesn't belong to him. Like the V.

This is one of the main reasons why I chose the title, *Power of the Vagina*, for this book. Some men believe that their personal power comes when a woman allows him to be in control, and she does whatever it is that he wants her to do. For example, take a pimp. A pimp feels powerless when they are unable to find females to work the streets for them. It isn't necessarily the money that gives a pimp his power; it's that the woman that agrees to release her body to the general public for sale and he controls her that gives a pimp his true power. Without the woman, there would be no power for a pimp. So, it goes back to the woman having the power to reproduce, and to make money. Of course, there are some men who offer their bodies for sale to lonely women, but it is primarily the women who control this industry.

I would like to share a story that was told to me some years ago. It's about a man and a woman who met each other, and decided to start dating one other a few years later. One thing led to another, and eventually they decided to move in together. Their relationship was as solid as a relationship can get for two people in love. Bill was thirty-one years old, and worked for a talent agency in Hollywood, California. His girlfriend Nancy, was twenty-six years old, and worked for a gas company. Neither one of them had any children. They attended church on Sunday mornings, and took in a movie on the weekends. Bill was the type of man who enjoyed doing a lot of work around the house. He was the handyman, and Nancy was what some would call a modern-day housewife, without being married or children to care for. She cleaned and cooked for the two of them; she also paid the bills, and made sure that their lives remained in order.

Bill and Nancy dated for nearly five years, and in those five years, they never once engaged in an argument with each other. Bill and Nancy were the typical American couple. Nancy liked sex, but Bill was in love with sex, in Bill's mind, he believed that Nancy's vagina belonged to him. Nancy didn't mind Bill's behavior. She even thought it was cute at times.

When Nancy would throw away a pair of her old panties, Bill would take her panties out of the trash, cut out the crotch area, put them in an empty plastic bag, and store them away. From time to time while he was alone, Bill would pull out his collection of Nancy's old panties and smell them. I know it may sound pretty sick to us, but Bill was truly in love with Nancy's vagina, and he didn't care who knew it.

Winter of 2007, Bill and Nancy were out shopping for Christmas gifts in downtown L.A., when a middle-aged man, standing at the bus stop, waiting for the bus, yelled out a comment to Nancy, as she and Bill walked down the street minding their own business. The man said, "Hey, girl! Why don't you share some of that vagina with a bro since its Christmas Eve? Ho! Ho! Ho!"

Bill heard the comment, and turned around.

"What did you say?" Bill asked the man.

"I wasn't talking to you, fool. I was talking to the lady you're with," the man answered.

"I asked you, what did you say to her?"

"It's none of your business I was talking to the lady."

"This lady belongs to me!" Bill yelled out at him, as Nancy stood there not far from where the man was standing.

"You gotta be crazy to think that she belongs to you," said the man.

"She belongs to me, like I said," Bill responded.

"Yeah, okay. Anyway, I asked the lady to share some of that vagina with me on Christmas Eve," said the man.

"I thought that was what you said. She's not going to share anything with you or anyone else. Like I said earlier, this is mine," said Bill.

"That vagina isn't yours. It's the lady's vagina. She can do whatever she wants to do with her vagina. If she chooses to share some of it with me then let her do that," said the man.

"Don't you ever disrespect me or my woman again," Bill said as he started to get angry.

"Are you willing to die over that vagina you call yours?" the man asked Bill as he stood there drinking an Olde English 800 beer.

"I'm willing to die, and I'm prepared to commit murder for this here vagina," Bill answered.

The man at the bus stop started to walk toward Bill and Nancy. He extended his hands out toward Nancy as he made comments to her.

"Come on, baby. Give papa some of that lovin. You know what I need. Give it to me, baby. You remember that song, don't you? That's the late great freaky Rick James song. Give me some of that Christmas Eve vagina," said the man.

Bill then pushed Nancy to the side, and pulled out a .357 Magnum handgun, and shot the man five times in the chest, killing him on the spot.

Nancy screamed, as she took the gun from Bill and threw it across the street, leaving one bullet in the chamber.

"WHAT DID YOU DO, BILL? WHY DID YOU SHOOT THAT MAN? HE WAS NOTHING, BUT A DRUNK. YOU SHOULD HAVE WALKED AWAY FROM HIM," Nancy screamed out.

"I shot him," Bill said in disbelief.

"You sure did," Nancy said.

"Is he dead?" Bill asked.

Nancy walked over to where the man lay in a puddle of blood. She checked his vital signs.

"He's dead! You killed an innocent man!" Nancy shouted out to Bill as she grabbed him by his shirt collar.

"I never meant to kill him," said Bill.

"We've got to call the police," said Nancy as she dialed 9-1-1 from her cell phone.

The police arrived at the scene they questioned Nancy, and several witnesses. They took Bill to the police station for questioning.

Nancy headed to her mother's house to tell her what happened. When she arrived at her mother's house, she ran inside straight to her mother's bedroom where she was watching television and drinking a hot cup of tea.

Nancy sat on the edge of her mother's bed, trying to compose herself; long enough to tell her mother what had just occurred. She cried so hard that her mother could barely understand her.

Nancy's mom sat there listening to the entire story before saying anything.

Nancy finally finished telling her mom what she had just witnessed.

After listening her mother replied "Nancy, It's a shame what happened to the man Bill murdered, and I feel sorry for Bill. Maybe the judge will find some leniency when it's time for him to be sentenced. Do you mind if I say a few words without you getting upset?"

"No Mom. Its fine, Say what it is you feel like saying. Personally, I'm all out of words," Nancy said as she laid her head on her mother's breast.

"I like Bill. 'She says as she comforts her daughter.' He is a hardworking man. He knows his position in the home, and he has no problem fixing things around the house. He even came by here and repaired a few things for me. Good man, but there is a side of him that I just don't care for. I saw how obsessed Bill became over you. Remember when you asked me to house-sit your place while you and Bill went on your vacation? I found some of your old panties with the crotch cut out of them. Then later while cleaning up, I found a brown paper bag with the crotch of your panties in single plastic Baggies, and when I looked in the brown paper bag there was a black book where Bill kept a journal of the dates he collected each panty. He wrote about how he would smell the crotch on days when he was alone. I knew then Bill had become obsessed with both you and your vagina. I knew that either someone would kill Bill, or Bill would end up murdering someone over your vagina. Look at what has happened tonight. A man who was drunk asked you to share your vagina on Christmas Eve, and because of that, Bill shot the man dead in the middle of the day, where there were hundreds of eyewitnesses. It all goes back to what my mother told me. If a man falls in love with the vagina, he might kill for it, and that is exactly what happened to your Bill. He was obsessed with your vagina."

Ask yourself: Was OJ obsessed with his ex-wife, Nicole Simpson? Could it have been his obsession for her that drove him to commit murder, or have her murdered? Could OJ have been so obsessed with Nicole, that in his mind, he started to say to himself, "If I can't have her, nobody else will?"

Many times people don't know if they are obsessed with someone until it's too late. History has shown us over and over, how someone can be obsessed with an actress to the point they either want to become them, or they stalk them. Obsession can cause a person to develop thoughts of suicide or thoughts of hurting someone else. Obsession can also make you powerless, and unable to resist the thought of being with out the person that consumes your every thought. This goes beyond "Love." Of course there are women who believe a man who calls all day, and wants to know your every move, etc., is showing her how much he cares about her, and how much he loves her. Some individuals may think that this type of conduct is how love, and the action of being in love are displayed, or that it is one in the same. I have a different opinion.

Love offers gentleness, affection, compassion, kind words, and soft kisses. Obsession offers staking, late night phone calls, gathering personal information and photos without permission. It can also includes showing up at your job, falling in love within days after meeting, staring you in your eyes without looking at anything, or anyone else, calling more than several times in a single day, and saving the glass you drank from, or old clothes you decided to throw away. There's a difference between love, and obsession. I strongly believe that every woman should know how to distinguish those differences. Remember that love and obsession are not the same.

Chapter Twenty

The Good, The Bad, and The Ugly V's

For years the rumor has been that some women have good vaginas, some have bad vaginas and believe it or not, some have ugly vaginas. As much as I don't want to talk about the ugly vagina, I feel it is my duty as a writer to discuss all three. I will start off talking about the ugly vagina.

Some women think they have a pretty vagina. Now, there really isn't a pretty vagina out there, especially when a vagina is wide open and you can see all of the small details and such. No offense, ladies, I'm only reporting what I have heard and seen for myself.

Just because you look like Halle Berry in the face, and have a Beyonce body, that does not mean you have a pretty vagina. Of course, you may shave your hair or cut a design into it, or have a pretty tattoo on the outside, but I'm talking about the inside.

I recall an incident back in 1983, when I met a young 23-year-old woman named Kim. She stood close to 5 feet 9 inches tall and weighed approximately 140 lbs. She had a caramel complexion with a coca cola body,

34-24-34. She was a true "Brick House." Well, one day she invited me over to her place to spend some time with her. When I got off work I headed over to Kim's house. When I arrived at her place she had left her front door slightly open. I slowly pushed the door open, walked inside and called out her name. The room was dark and music was playing. I heard Kim's voice say, "Come into the bedroom, John."

I walked towards the direction of room where the voice came from, it was Kim's bedroom. When I walked into the room the lights were on, and Kim was lying in the middle of the bed with her legs wide open with nothing on. Her pubic hair was all shaved off and she left nothing to the imagination. I had a clear vision of what Kim's vagina looked like outside and inside before ever having sex with her. She lay there smiling.

I stood at the foot of the bed and thought to myself. Damn her vagina looks like a 90 year-old, dried up, beat up, wrinkled prune, lying in the middle of the sand. That is what her vagina looked like to me. There was no way in hell I was going to have sex with that thing, I was thinking as I stood at the foot of the bed.

"What are you waiting for, John?" Kim asked.

"Nothing," I answered as I reached for my beeper and triggered it to go off, Beep! Beep! Beep! Beep! Beep! I looked down at my pager and looked at a number that I had already returned in fact, it was her number. I had called her to tell her that I was on my way. Anyway I said to Kim, "I'm sorry. This is my grandmother paging me. She just had a stroke. I need to get to her house right away. I'll call you later."

"I understand, John. You better get going," said Kim, as she appeared to be concerned about my grandmother.

I left Kim's house and I never returned or called her again.

Man that was one ugly vagina.

Now that I have told you about the ugly vagina, let's talk about the bad vagina.

A woman that has a bad vagina is one that does bad things with it. For example, a woman with a bad vagina is someone who uses her vagina to have babies, and get on welfare for the money and food stamps. A woman with a bad vagina will get pregnant by someone she hates, and turn him into the district attorney's child support division. When, in most cases, the child doesn't even belong to the man that is accused of being the father. The woman with the bad vagina will go out and have sex with different men in the same night, and not once will she take a shower or bathe before changing partners. We could also call this vagina, a "Nasty Vagina." A Bad Vagina will be infected with a STD and pass it on to other men without them knowing. She will also let her lover go down on her and smile while he's down there doing his thing. A Bad Vagina can smell like ten-day-old fish and not have any concerns about the smell. A Bad Vagina will ask her partner to perform oral sex on her while she's on her period.

This is the kind of vagina that every man needs to stay away from. Just like "all money isn't good money." "All vagina isn't good vagina."

Lastly, I would like to discuss the good vagina.

I decided to save the best for last.

Now we come to the good vagina. The woman with the good vagina has morals, respect and responsibilities. Every six months she's at her doctor's office having a routine checkup. A good vagina could come with an unattractive face and a torn-up body. Most men identify a pretty face and a nice body as someone with a "Good Vagina," when in fact they may have only seen the woman on videos or in a magazine. A man shouldn't pass judgment based on looks.

If a man is hungry, spoiled food will taste good to him. A man that isn't hungry gets to choose his food, because only beggars can't be choosey when they're hungry.

If a man has sex with a woman he deeply desires, of course to him her vagina will appear to be good.

I believe it's not what a woman looks like that determines if she has a good, bad or ugly V. It's more about how that woman makes her partner feel. I used this example to demonstrate that we should not look at the V as being an object or tool, but more like an opportunity to experience a joyful moment with what God has given to women. Just because the V is good doesn't mean it can't be "ugly." Just because the V is ugly doesn't mean it can't be good, and just because the V doesn't perform the way one might expect doesn't mean it can't be good.

Question ladies:

"What does a good vagina feel like?"
"What does a bad vagina smell like?
"What does an ugly vagina look like?

Just curious.

Chapter Twenty- One

The Restricted V

You may read this story and think it is about a young woman who decides to become celibate after her husband is sent to federal prison. The truth to this story isn't about the love of her life going to prison. It's about a young woman who believes in morals, values, and her wedding vows. This scenario is a demonstration of true strength, faith, and belief including the use of "Mind over Matter." Many of you may take this cliché for granted, but I strongly believe there is a lot of truth to this statement. Of course, some individuals find it difficult to use their mind to control a simple matter.

"I sentence you to 240 months to the Bureau of Prison, for the distribution of one hundred and twenty-five Kilos of Cocaine across the State line," said a Los Angeles, Federal Judge on the morning of December 8, 2008.

As this young man by the name of Alvin Blackstone received that sentence, his wife Lisa was sitting at home waiting by the telephone for her husband to call. The telephone barely rang once before Lisa answered.

"Hello," Lisa answers the phone anxiously.

"This is a collect call from Alvin, an inmate from a Federal Prison. You will not be charged for this call. To accept this call, press five, or press seven to block this call," said a pre-recorded operator.

Lisa quickly presses the number five button to accept Alvin's call.

"Hello baby," says Alvin.

Lisa replies, don't 'baby me. I've been sitting here worried half to death. I haven't eaten all day. I am so nervous I have been running back and forth to the bathroom. What took you so long to call, and why are you calling me from prison? What happened in court today?"

"Baby, they sentenced me to two hundred and forty months."

"240 MONTHS! How much time is that?"

"Its twenty years, love."

"Oh no, Alvin are you kidding me? Twenty years! I thought the lawyer said that you would only get, at the most, probation. Twenty damn years! THAT'S NOT RIGHT. You haven't killed anybody, and you haven't molested any kids. A child molester can kidnap and rape a child and only get seven years. A drunk driver can run into an entire family of five, kill everyone in the car, and only get seven years. WHY, WHY,WHY, TWENTY YEARS!" Lisa breaks down.

Alvin attempts to comfort her. "It's going to be ok baby; please don't cry. I need for you to be strong baby. You're going to have to step into both of our shoes, and be the provider until I can figure something out, and I will figure something out."

Lisa breaks down.

Then she asks, "Did the judge say anything about the money that is in trust for the kids?"

"They confiscated the whole trust."

"The entire six hundred and seventy thousand dollars, How can they do that?"

"They are the Feds. Remember, my indictment said, 'The United States of America,' versus Alvin Blackstone! It was me against the whole damn United States of America, but believe me it's not the end of the world."

"I just want you to know that I'm going to wait the whole twenty years for you. It's you and me until the wheels fall off the car baby. I mean that from the bottom of my heart. I love you, believe me when I took my vows, twenty one years ago, I said 'I do' to everything, which means if you're in prison, so am I."

"I'm sure after a few years have gone by you'll find someone to take my place."

"Like I said, if you're in prison, then I'm in prison, so don't you worry, and that's including my vagina. I'm going to place her on restriction while you're away." Lisa says as she tries to make light out of this extremely serious situation.

The very next day, Lisa returned to work. There she met up with two of her closest friends and co-workers who were on break.

Her friend Lillie says, "Give up the 4-1-1."

"It wasn't good. They sentenced Alvin to two hundred and forty months." Lisa answered.

Lillie sighs and says, "Damn, they sentenced Alvin to twenty years? That is a long time."

Judy adds, "A very long time."

Lisa put her finger to her lips and quietly says, "Lower your voice. I don't want the whole office to hear that my husband is in prison."

Judi asks her, "What are you going to do?"

Lisa says "Do about what, my mortgage and my kid's tuition? I have no idea, but one thing I do know, I'm not going to mess around with any other men while my husband is away."

"What are you saying; are you really thinking about placing your vagina on restriction for twenty years?" Lillie asks.

"Yes, I'm willing to do that for my husband."

"You know," Lillie says, "I'm not sure I would wait twenty years. However, I could probably wait a good three to five years if, and only if, we were married before he went to prison."

"Judi adds her two cents, "Let my man take his ass to prison and see if I'll wait for him. I'm not waiting a day. I refuse to place my precious vagina on restriction for any long period of time. The vagina was not meant to be placed on restriction."

In the story above, Lisa is willing to remain celibate for the man she loves. Her friend, Judi, refuses to wait 24 hours. To restrict yourself is to deny yourself from the things that bring pleasure into your life, whether we're talking about chocolate, food, or sex. I believe, if a woman decides that her man is worthy of celibacy, and she decides to deny herself from doing what she enjoys for a reason that makes sense to her. That is her decision.

Restriction sometimes means you give up your rights and choices for another human being. You surely must ask yourself, is my partner worth me going without. This can be extremely tricky for married couples because their vows say, "For better or worse." For your husband to be sentenced to twenty years in prison is definitely "for worse." Of course this is the ultimate test for someone who is married, and his or her significant other goes away for a long period of time. Your heart may tell you to wait, and your mind may tell you to wait, but the sex organ has a voice of its own. It may say something totally differently, because it is that part of the body that has become addicted to the joyful aroused feeling it experiences while you are engaged in sexual intercourse. So, ask yourself this before you say I do. "Will I be able to place myself on restriction should something happen to my partner?" This will prove the love you have for your husband or wife.

Now, let's observe Lisa's friend Judi. Judi made it perfectly clear that she wouldn't wait 24 hours for a man if he went to jail. Does this make Judi a bad person? Of course not, we all have a choice in life and her choice is not to place herself on restriction like Lisa. I am sure that the majority of married women didn't consider that their vows would include the words, 'for better or worse, richer or poorer, in sickness and in health, til death do us part and til release from prison. This means as long as her husband, Alvin is on lock down so is her vagina. Lisa's friend Judi is entitled to make a decision about her own relationship.

Now as for Lisa, she's one of a kind, and I am speaking from experience. There are not very many women who will place themselves on restriction and not have sex for that long of a time. Most women will go out on dates, have phone conversations, and go on with their lives while you're doing twenty years in federal prison.

The mother of my two children told me if I went to prison that she would wait, but she didn't. Hell, after I was sentenced and transferred to Yazoo, Mississippi back in May 2001, it only took a few months before it was over. The letters and cards came to a halt. The calls I placed to her were not being accepted some of the time, and as for visitation, I never saw her again. Our relationship lasted for fifteen years with two children, but that time doesn't mean a thing when you take your ass off to prison for a long period of time. Do I believe that Lisa being only forty years old will wait for twenty years? Only time will tell. It takes a special, and I mean a *special* lady to wait that long for any man, especially if she's not married to him. Where there is no commitment or love there will be no waiting and that you can take to the bank. I recall what my mother and youngest sister said to me the day after I found out my woman had moved on with her life. "Son, ten years is a long time, Lord knows it is, and this is the time for you to pray and ask the Lord to watch over you. As far as Denise is concerned, let her go, because I don't see her waiting ten years for you or any other man." And I feel the same way my mama feels. My woman was only thirty-two years old and still young. Now, if she is seventy-two you might have a chance of her waiting.

For those women who decide to restrict themselves and wait for their man or husband, I commend you, especially if you have a good man. Just because someone goes to prison doesn't make him or her bad person. All it means is that the man or woman made a bad decision. Judge that man or woman by their character, and how they treat you as a human being, and if you wish to place yourself on restriction because you have someone that is worth it, then you do that and hope for the best.

Chapter Twenty-Two

The Abused V

Just when I thought this book was complete, I received a telephone call from a friend of one of my friends. She wanted to speak with me regarding an abusive relationship she was involved in. Of course I was sympathetic, so try to be understanding particularly when it comes to this topic.

She began to share her story with me about how she has endured physical abuse for the past two years from the man she believed loved her. Let me take you back to the day she called.

I was driving down the highway when my cell phone rang. It was a private number. Now, I usually don't answer private numbers, but for some reason I answered this one.

"Hello."

"May I speak to John, please?" It was a female voice.

"This is John. Who's speaking?"

"You don't know me. My name is Lela and I got your number from Jamie."

"Yea, I know Jamie. How can I help you?"

"Are you busy, should I call back later?"

"No, I can talk. Actually I'm driving, so I have a few minutes. What can I do for you?" 'Yes I had my earpiece attached.'

"Jamie told me about the book you're writing and she suggested that I speak with you about my relationship."

I asked, "Is it just a relationship or is there more to it?"

"There's more to it, and this is hard for me to say." She paused, took a deep breath and said, "I've been living in an abusive relationship for the past two years and I have pretty much kept it a secret."

I asked, "What makes it a secret?"

"Because Jamie is the only one that knows, not even my mother knows, and she and I are closer than my sisters and me. When he beats me, I don't visit anyone; I stay in the house, sometimes, for days until the swelling goes down. I can't do much about the black eyes." She started to cry.

I asked "Are you okay?"

"Yes, I am alright, considering my circumstance."

"So why do you stay?" I asked.

"I stay because I'm in love with him."

I replied, "There are a whole lot of men out here who you can fall in love with and it won't include a beat down to be with them. Do you have any kids?"

"Two."

"By the guy who abuses you?"

"She sighs then answers, "Yes, which is another reason why I don't want to leave him. My kids would be left without a father in their lives."

I asked her, "how can he possibly be a positive influence in your kids' life when he is an abusive husband, when did he start to beat you?"

She replied, "The first five years were perfect. We never had an argument or disagreement. Our relationship seemed like it was something out of a book of fairy tales, but when we got married two years ago, the relationship went downhill from that point on, and he suddenly became abusive."

My next question was, "Did you ever notice any signs of violence? Did he make jokes about hitting you, or killing you if he caught you messing around with another man?"

"I can't recall." Then after a few seconds of silence she said, "Wait, I can recall a few times when he talked about slapping, and kicking me until I threw up blood, but I thought he was joking. I also noticed how his attitude changed when he got angry with his boss or one of his family members, but I didn't think anything of it."

I said, "Most women who are physically abused don't think anything of it. You all seem to think that it's all fun and games when your man tells you things like he is going to slap you, or kick you until you throw up blood."

"But he tells me he loves me," she interrupted

"And . . . ."

"And, I believe him."

"Tell me how many times your husband abused you?"

"More times than I care to remember, it's happened quite a few times."

"Did you report this abuse to the authorities; do you have a police report on file?" I asked.

"No. I'm not trying to send my husband to jail for something I've done."

"Listen I don't know you, but I suggest that you leave him, not tomorrow, not later today but right now. Please consider the advice I have given you and get help for yourself and your children."

"Thank you for taking the time to listen to what I had to say. It was nice talking with you."

I say goodbye and we end our call.

The above story is typical of women who are victims of physical abuse. Abused women are inclined to believe they are the cause of the abuser's anger or madness. In this type of relationship the man manipulates the woman's mind. He starts to become a CONTROLLER in the relationship instead of a COMPANION. There are usually signs and patterns from the abuser that the woman chooses to either ignore or make excuses for. For many years women in abusive relationships have stayed because of love, fear, the kids, or a combination of things. Some women even believe that a man who hits them it is just showing an expression of love.

What many women don't know is this, a man who becomes angry, and he doesn't put his hands on them is considered normal in any relationship. When a man becomes "Mad" this is a whole different display of anger. Human beings get angry, animals get mad, animals fight and they often kill their victim. Is love supposed to inflict pain? Hell no! This woman is like millions of other women who live in these same circumstances, but chose to stay in their violent relationship. This usually comes from low-self esteem or no self-esteem at all.

Most victims of abuse fail to pay attention to the subtle warning signs of an abuser. Before an abuser becomes physical he usually is controlling. He has to have something to use before attacking his victim. Let me give you an example; if he says to you. "This is your third time coming home late from work. You must be seeing somebody behind my back. Are you cheating on me? Have you screwed some other man besides me?" What he's doing is building up his anger so he feels justified for attacking you.

Abusers usually don't wake up in the morning and just beat the living crap out of his victim. It usually comes from a thought in his conscious mind. The victim can be totally innocent; it doesn't matter if he is your man or husband. While writing this chapter I have come to find out that most abusers have been abused themselves, or they have witnessed their mother being abused by their father or stepfather. The male that sees this in his home usually repeats this type of behavior. When an act like this plays out for years, in his mind this is normal conduct, so when he grows up he starts to re-enact what he has witnessed, as a child, on his girlfriend or spouse. This is not all cases; there are men who have promised themselves that they would never hit a woman because of what they have seen their mother, sister or aunt endure while growing up.

One of the questions I ask victims is, "how do you know you're in a relationship with an abuser?" They all have the same answer. "You don't."

An abuser doesn't walk around with a t-shirt on with the word "ABUSER" printed on it, and they don't have tattoos or ankle bracelets labeling them as an abuser.

An abuser usually is kind, respectful, and caring in the beginning of their relationship, which can give any woman the illusion that they have found Mr. Right or her Soul Mate. Later it is discovered that they are in love with an abuser, you see an abuser waits for the right time to show his true colors.

If what I have said, you find to be true, or that this holds any truth to it; such as 'he waits to become angry', gets mad for no reason before attacking', then you may want to consider making him a little angry as a test run. I would rather hear that some man cussed you out and called you every name in the book. I do not want to hear that you're in the hospital with a broken rib or fighting for your life because you have been attacked by your abuser.

I hope this chapter will bring light into that dark place in many women's lives. Especially those women who are living in this type of relationship, God made other men, who also have a penis if that is what is keeping you attached to an abusive relationship.

When you go out on dates, ask questions. Find out if that man grew up in an abusive home or if he has ever been abused, as a child, by his parents or parent. Ask him if he ever hit a woman before or thought about hitting a woman. Ask him how he handles his anger when he becomes angry. Ask about his relationship with his own mother. Is he close to her? Is he a "Mama's Boy?" Did she spoil him when he was a child, and does he expect the same from his woman or wife if he ever gets married? Ask him about his father and his feelings for him. A man that carries hatred in his heart for his father could be a man that doesn't know how to forgive and forget. This can be a bad sign if he can't because, believe me, there will be a time when you and your man are going to get into an argument over something. If he holds anger in his heart because of his father being absent in his life, you may want to think about the times when you may be absent because of weekend trips with your girlfriends or family members, or you may be away for more than a weekend.

It is much better to detach yourself from someone who you never really got to know, and hold no emotional feelings for, than to wait until you fall head over heels and it's too late. It's hard to detach yourself from a person when emotions have set in your heart. It becomes; "Easier said than done." Walk away from it before anything strong develops. Walk away from what you might think is love. If you feel in your mind that something is wrong with this picture, or if you get that funny feeling in your gut that many people often feel, DON'T IGNORE IT.

As for Lela and her abuser in the above story, I received a call from Jamie several days later after speaking with Lela and was told that Lela's abuser took her life.

Don't become a victim; get away while you still can.

Chapter Twenty-Three

The V Keeper

I've come to realize that most men are looking for that "Vagina Keeper" (V.K.). The one that makes a man say those two words, "I Do," and those other two words that follows "I Do," "I Will" I will love her until death do us part, I will protect her, I will encourage her, I will support her, I will respect her and I will never divorce her. I, too, feel that same way.

Unfortunately, they just don't raise women (or men!) the way they use to when I was growing up. A Vagina Keeper is a woman that will love you regardless of whether or not you're able to run a marathon. If you are paralyzed from the waist down, if you won the lottery and became the next millionaire, or if you fell on hard times sleeping on skid row, she will still love you.

When a person cares for you deeply, it surpasses what being in love supposedly represents. Having deep love for a man allows the woman to love him in spite of all his flaws, bad habits, and addictions. In order to deeply love someone you must look past their outer appearance. In the book of Proverbs

31:30, it tells us not to base love on the beauty of a woman but on her character, instead.

A Vagina Keeper isn't based on how a woman performs in bed or in the back seat of a car. She's the whole package; a real V.K. isn't only dressed on the outside, but on the inside as well. Her character becomes her clothes and shoes, and her integrity becomes her lipstick and make-up. I believe a woman's beauty and looks is only her initial introduction to who she is; her beauty goes beyond what we can see. We can dress up a pig but it doesn't mean that pig is no longer pork.

Many of you may be saying to yourselves, "What is the difference between a V.K. and a wife?" They are one in the same. According to the Bible it says: "Wives must submit themselves to their husband, for a husband has authority over his wife. A wife needs to respect her husband."

Of course, when a man finds a V.K., he completely submits himself to that woman because all of his needs, wants, and desires are being met. Let's take a man's needs: When a man's needs are being met, he usually won't leave or cheat on his woman, but when a man begins to have "Wants" this is where he starts to question his relationship. A human being has a need for water, food and air. We as human creatures are never satisfied with what we have; we tend to always want more. For example, take a man that doesn't have a car at all and someone gives him a raggedy 1985 Hyundai, he will be content because his *needs* are being met and he has no *wants* or *desires* for anything else. He is grateful. Now take a man that owns that same raggedy 1985 Hyundai, but *wants* a brand new Lexus, he will never be content with his Hyundai until he gets what he *wants*, even though his *needs* are being met. Now if a man has a *desire* for a Ferrari, a car that cost five times what the average middle class blue-collar worker earns in a year, and he's able to purchase that Ferrari, then his *desire* has been satisfied.

Looking at the above examples, his *needs, wants,* and *desires* have all been met. Now take those same examples and use them in a man and woman relationship. If a man only has *needs* from his woman and his *needs* are being met, eight out of ten times, he will remain faithful in his relationship because he doesn't have any *wants* or *desires* to fulfill. A man who is getting sex four days a week from his woman but *wants* to have sex seven days a week is not going to be content until his *wants* are met, even though his *needs* are being met.

Then you have a man who *desires* to have a three-some with his woman and she is willing to fulfill his *desire.* He is satisfied and content because of her wiliness to meet his *needs, wants* and *desire.* Ten out of ten without any doubt, a man has truly found his soul mate and she's definitely a V.K. for life. The majority of men cheat, creeps, or commits adultery in a relationship when a *need, want,* or *desire* is not being met by his partner and for no other reason.

Since this book was written for women, the choice becomes the womans' and the choices that you all make in life become your happiness or regrets.

A woman that knows her true worth knows in her heart that she's a Vagina Keeper and at no time will she have a need to settle for anything less. The last thing a woman wants is to wake up one morning after being married for several years is to realize that she was the only one married in the relationship.

"How do I become a Vagina Keeper uncle?" one of my nieces asked me one Saturday when I spoke with her on the phone while I was writing this chapter. I sat my pen down for a moment and I thought about her question. I knew whatever I told her, it would affect her for the rest of her life regarding men and relationships. I knew that she was counting on me to guide her in making the right choices when it concerns relationships and marriage. "Grab a pen and a piece of paper. I'm going to tell you exactly what you need to know, and how to prepare yourself in becoming a Vagina Keeper."

"Here's a list you should keep on your refrigerator and read it every day," I said. I proceeded to give her the V.K. list over the phone.

A. The first thing is that a Vagina Keeper must be completely happy with self and realize that happiness isn't based on having a man in your life.

B. Have the confidence of a queen, and know that it is you who holds the power.

C. Know what true love consists of before you give your heart to some man and you really don't know the first thing about love.

D. Stop exposing so much of yourself for men to see. More isn't always better. Leave something to the imagination. Most gifts are wrapped, so be a gift to a man.

E. Prepare yourself to be a wife, a woman with integrity that has self-respect, and love for yourself as well as others. Be open minded, a good listener, save yourself for your soul-mate and have a good heart.

F. Learn how to control your own sexual needs, wants, and desires by choosing mental stimulation instead of having sex. Don't jump into bed with just any guy because your hormones have kicked in.

G. Communicate without sexual flirting or sexual innuendo.

H. Be willing to share your space and time. A selfish woman can never be a Vagina Keeper.

I. If a man's needs, wants, and desires make you feel uncomfortable, angry or insecure, GET OUT OF THE RELATIONSHIP! Trust your feelings. If it feels wrong to you, it IS wrong. Period.

Last, be willing to meet all the man's needs, wants and desires within reason—and make sure he is willing to meet yours within reason, too. If a man's needs, wants or desires aren't being met, he will creep elsewhere to have them fulfilled.

"To the real Vagina Keepers, make yourselves visible!"

Chapter Twenty-Four

The American Dream V

SATURDAY NIGHT 9:22 P.M.
MY PLACE

What constitutes an American Dream Vagina? That is what I asked myself one Saturday night as I sat at my computer trying to decide what to write for my next chapter. Unlike all of the other chapters I had an idea of exactly what I wanted to write about in this one.

I decided to get up from the computer, take a shower, and put on some clothes and head out to one of the hottest nightclubs in Hollywood to interview some party girls. There I felt I would find the answers I needed to complete this chapter. After years of dating and never marrying, I wanted to search for what makes an American Dream Vagina, which in my opinion is the same as a wife. Men tend to believe that as long as a woman can cook, keep the house clean, raise our children, organize the household and provide us with sex that is the making of a good wife. Of course I have a different viewpoint now that I have written this book about women.

That evening I interviewed eleven women of different ages and nationalities but before that night ended I would have an encounter that would change my life forever.

SATURDAY NIGHT 11:01 PM

I stood in the VIP line along with approximately one hundred other people that were waiting to get into the club. One of the doormen recognized me as he lifted up the red velvet rope and let me through. I made my way to the front of the crowded line and got to the cashiers window where a middle age Italian woman was sitting behind a glass window. Her job was to collect the cover charge and issue VIP wristbands to certain people.

I handed the cashier a fifty-dollar bill and waited for my change.

"Is this your first time here?" she asked, as she handed me my change.

"Yes it is I'm actually here to see Steve."

"Would your name be John?"

"Yes, I'm John."

"He's expecting you. Let me give you a VIP wristband, without it you will not be able to get inside of the VIP room. He loves hanging out with the celebrities. Steve actually thinks he's a celebrity at times," she said as she placed the VIP wristband around my wrist.

"Thank you."

"Make a left turn as soon as you pass the double doors then make a quick right at the stairs, there you will see a guy wearing an all black suit. Show him your wristband. He will let you into the VIP room. You have a nice time."

"I'm sure I will and thanks again," I replied.

I made it inside the VIP room. There were people everywhere, actresses, actors, movie producers, music producers, rappers, and hundreds of models standing around talking, drinking, and dancing. I stood near the front door for a minute before making my way toward the bar. I wanted to check out the scenery from a distance, so I decided to walk over to the bar to order myself something to drink.

"May I take your order sir?" a male bartender asked.

"Yes, I'll have a glass of orange juice with ice."

"With a shot of . . . ?"

"Nothing, I don't drink alcohol, plain orange juice will be just fine."

"One orange juice on the rocks coming up, your first time here?" the bartender asked.

"Yes it's my first time here; I'm actually looking for the club owner Steve."

"That's Steve right over there," the bartender points. "He's surrounded by a group of wanna-be actresses and models. You may not be able to see Steve. He's no taller than 5'2 maybe 5'3 when he's wearing his plat-form shoes. Just follow the crowd, that's where you will find him," said the bartender.

I made my way through the crowd to find him. I noticed a crowd of females surrounding someone, so I went in that direction, and there was Steve standing in the center of the crowd wearing a two piece black suit, a light blue cotton shirt with a large unlit cigar hanging from his mouth. I knew that he had to be him because the bartender said he was short, he had a bottle of Grey Goose in his right hand. I approached him.

"Excuse me, are you Steve?"

"Yes, I'm Steve, and you are?"

"I'm John, we spoke earlier I'm the writer."

"Oh yea, yea, I remember talking to you, I believe you said you were writing a book about the vagina is that correct?"

"That's correct, I was wondering if I could interview a few of the young ladies in the house tonight."

"Take your pick as you can see there's plenty to choose from, and there's another six hundred or so downstairs."

"I only need to speak with eleven."

"No problem let me see. I chose that one in the pink shear lace dress with no underwear or bra. The one over there in the black two piece skirt set. That one right there with the huge fake breasts. The one near the front door by the bar that's leaning over showing all of her assets is cool. Those two ladies right there in the white pants suits, the four girls sitting at the cocktail table sitting alone and the one over there looking like a young J-Lo."

I waited near the bar and within minutes, Steve had directed all eleven ladies over to where I was standing. The bartender opened the room for us. Everyone took a seat and I introduced myself to them. "Hello Ladies, my name is John Watts and I'm sure you are wondering why you're here in this dark, dirty room. Well, I'm a writer and I wanted to speak with a group of young ladies to see if I could get some answers about a particular chapter for a book I'm writing. This is my reason for being here tonight, is that okay with you ladies?"

Simultaneously, the women all said yes.

"I would like to start from my left. I will go around and ask each of you your name and age, starting with you. What's your name and age?"

"My name is Pam, and I'm 21."

"My name is Anna, and I'm 23."

"My name is Connie, and I'm 25."

"My name is Bessie and I'm 24."

"My name is Dolla, I'm 23."

"My name is Zola, and I'm 29."

"My name is Tameika, I'm 21."

"My name is Jen and I'm 21."

"My name is Sandra, I'm 40."

"My name is Kim Hung, and I am 22."

"And my name is Jalapeno and I'm 23."

"My name is John Watts, I am a Writer, and I am currently writing a new book called "Power of the Vagina.""

"You got the right one, baby, right here look no further," Pam shouted out as she raised her breast with her hands and smiled.

"She may be the right one, but I'm the best one." said Dolla

Lola stood up and posed for me as she raised her blouse to show her 44 double D size breast.

"Okay Lola, I get the point you're trying to make, but I'm not here for a breast contest. I'm here looking for the answer to my one question."

"What is the one question John?" Bessie asked.

"I would like to start with Pam. Pam how would you describe an American Dream Vagina?"

"How would I describe an American Dream Vagina, you're looking at her," said Pam.

"I need words, not a picture. Let's try using w-o-r-d-s Pam, if you could. Everyone, language please, describe an American Dream Vagina."

"I would have to say it's a combination of things. It's not just one thing. It's her eyes, her hair, her breast and of course her vagina," Pam answered.

"I see your answer is based around the body parts of a woman. Describe an American Dream Vagina, Anna?"

"It's all about the way a woman performs in bed. Every man on earth would like to have sex with a woman that knows what she's doing in the bed and a woman that looks like Pamela Anderson. She's the American Dream Vagina."

"So it's all about how she performs in bed and if she looks like Pamela Anderson." I asked.

"Yes. She's an American Icon in my book." said Anna.

"Okay and you Connie?"

"An American Dream Vagina, in my opinion, is a woman that holds power and I'm not talking about power between her legs, I'm talking about the power between her ears. Women like Oprah, Condoleezza, Tyra, Hilary, Mrs. Shriver and First Lady Michelle Obama." Connie answered.

"So powerful women are the American Dream Vagina in your opinion?" I asked Connie once again.

"That is correct. If I were a man, which I'm not, those would be the type of women I would be going after. Not the Tameika's, Bessie's or Lula's. I'm just giving those six ladies their prop that's all. When I think of an American Dream Vagina, I think of them." Connie answered.

"Good answer Connie, damn good answer. I'm impressed, believe it or not. And you Bessie, what is your answer?"

"I was raised by my stepmother and she taught me that, the vagina only makes up half of a woman, the other half is her mouth," Bessie answered.

"So your stepmother taught you. What comes out of a woman's mouth is what makes her a complete woman?" I asked.

"No she taught me what goes in a woman's mouth makes her a complete woman," Bessie answered.

"Okay, Bessie, well taught by step mom. What about you Dolla. What did your stepmother teach you?" I asked.

"I didn't have a Stepmother; however my mother did teach me a few things. First of all, an American Dream Vagina goes deeper than what the eyes can see. An American Dream Vagina is a vagina that places herself on hold while searching for her soul mate," Dolla replied.

"So, if a woman has already had sex once, twice or a thousand times before she finds her soul mate, she could never be an American Dream Vagina in your eyes?" I asked.

"This is absolutely correct. How could a whore be an American Dream Vagina when a thousand penises have already been inside of her?" Dolla asked me.

"Are you saying a woman must be a virgin?" I asked.

"I am. A real American man is not looking for a whore. Could a man teach a whore how to become a housewife?" Dolla answered as she sat there on a bar stool sipping her Apple Martini.

"Thank you for your answer. Zola, what is your answer?"

"I believe an American Dream Vagina is a woman who has her own home or condo, her own money, her own car, a high FICA score and a good job," Zola answered.

"So an independent woman is what makes up an American Dream Vagina?"

"That's part of it. The other part is when a woman doesn't need anything from a man and that includes his penis,"

"I take it, you're a lesbian?" I asked.

"A proud lesbian and I believe lesbians are the true American Dream Vagina."

"And why do you believe that?" I asked.

"For so many years, men have made us women a second class citizen. We have always taken the back seat, but times are changing. We're now equal to the man and in the next fifty years, we will be the trailblazers of America," Zola answered as she stood up and posed in front of everyone with her hands on her hips, waiting for someone to make a comment.

"A person should stand up for what they believe in, whether it's right or wrong. Now for you, Ms. Tameika, are you a lesbian, too?" I asked.

"No I'm not; this is all woman, baby. In fact, a woman can't do anything for me in the bedroom," Tameika answered.

"So what makes a woman an American Dream Vagina and I'm sure you have a good answer for me being that you're the only black woman in the bunch," I asked.

"I have an answer but I don't know how good it is. Describe an American Dream Vagina. Okay an American Dream Vagina is a vagina that is free from STD's, HIV/AIDS, a vagina that's tight and doesn't smell like spoiled butter milk. That is the American Dream Vagina, oh and a vagina that knows how to please a man in bed," Tameika answered.

"So it's all about the vagina?" I asked

"It's all about the vagina and how good you can work it, that's the difference between me and the other ten ladies in this room. If there was a ten most wanted list, my vagina would be on it," said Tameika.

"The ten most wanted list for the worst vagina in the State of California," Pam shouts out and everyone laughed.

"Let's stay on point ladies. I didn't come here to see a cat fight."

A white female raised her hand.

"Yes?" I asked.

"I believe I'm next."

"And tell me your name again."

"My name is Sandra."

"Go ahead Sandra. Answer the question."

"An American Dream Vagina is a vagina that can get a man that wants to be in a serious relationship. It also has the capability to find a man that wants to spend the rest of his life with the woman, and never commit adultery or cheat on her. If your stuff can catch a husband, you have an American Dream Vagina or that "Bomb Bay Coochie," as my girl Tameika puts it, but if your stuff can't find that husband or soul mate, you may want to evaluate yourself. You may just have the type of vagina that only has the capability to satisfy a man for the moment and not a life time. This type of man can find that anytime. It is a dime a dozen. There's plenty of that type of vagina right here in this room and in this club."

"Hold up, wait a minute! Everybody might not want a husband. That doesn't mean she's got some no good coochie," Tameika shouts out.

Dolla shouts, "Tameika is right."

Bessie shouted "She is right, Sandra. A woman can have some good vagina or coochie, whatever you choose to call it and just wishes to remain single."

Sandra says, "Just like the early bird catches the worm. Good vagina catches the husband, or it catches more than a one night stand. I rest my case."

Zola says, "I hate when she does that, but maybe this time she's right."

"Actually, I like the answer you gave, Sandra. Kim Hung, do you have a better answer than, Sandra?" I asked.

"I believe I do have an answer that would actually come as a shock to you guys for a Korean woman. Korean vaginas are usually tight, unlike some of you American women. We didn't have sex very much in our country, at least not women over the age of forty. The story is different for us Korean women here in America. Now Korean women have been transformed, and between the ages of twenty and thirty, we are having sex just as much as American women if not more. For many years, the Korean women would remain silent while having sex. They were not allowed to say a word in bed. They also only engaged in two positions, on their back or doggy style. You would never catch a Korean woman climbing on top of a Korean man and as far as oral sex goes, that is simply unheard of in our country. We were taught that oral sex was dirty. The new breeds of Korean young ladies here in America and a few in our country are performing oral sex. I've been in America for three years and I have learned things I never knew. I let my man slap my ass and flip me around the room and my favorite position is on top. Do you know there are millions of Korean women that have never experienced an orgasm?"

"Zola interrupts her and says, "Girl that doesn't just happen to Korean women, that happens to all of us."

"We Korean women are very shy. So, when you ask me to describe an American Dream Vagina, the only thing I could base that question on is what my forty year old brother told me not long ago. He said that he has had sex with Korean, Caucasian and African American women, and the best vagina of the three was the African American woman. So, my answer is an African American woman. She is the American Dream Vagina," Kim Hung answered.

Tameika jumped up and screamed out loud. "That's what I'm talking about. Once you go black you will never turn back. The black vagina is the American Dream Vagina. I rest my case."

"Thank you Kim, Jen it's your turn."

Jen says, "First I want to say that I love the title of your book. It reminds me so much of myself. Well for starters, I have to agree with Kim Hung and Connie's answers. I'm old enough and wise enough to know, you need to bring more than a piece of vagina into a relationship in order to find a decent man. What a real man expects his woman or his wife to know is the basics. How to cook a meal, keep a house clean, pay bills, balance a check book, and how to get off her tail and go to work, if needed, in order to make ends meet. I'm not saying that the vagina doesn't play a role in all this. A woman needs to know how to use it; there are a lot of women who don't know the first thing about how to please a man. They feel as long as the man reaches a climax he's satisfied. Let me share this story with you ladies. I have a girlfriend named Marie. She's a few years older than me. She use to make her man "boo-boo" in the bed while having sex, that's what you call pleasing your man. When you get to that level I believe that is the ultimate pleasure for a man. I'm not saying one has to go around making men "boo-boo" on themselves but it would definitely let him know who's in charge. My friend, Marie is the American Dream Vagina."

"Is that your final answer, Jen?" I asked.

"I would also like to add that I too have that American Dream Vagina,"

"And what makes your vagina that American Dream Vagina?" I asked

"Because I have that pop," she said.

"Pop?" Bessie shouted out.

"Yes. Jen says I have that smack, crackle, and Pop."

"Oh, so you only have the 'pop' without the "smack and the crackle," Zola asked Jen.

"Correct, Zola," Jen answered

Zola says "24 hours with me. I'll teach you how to make that thing go, smack, crackle and pop."

Jen says. "No thank you, Zola. I don't do the lesbian thing. In fact, my pussy is actually allergic to other bitches pussies". You got me twisted.

Everyone laughed, including me.

"Thanks, Jen. Would you like to give an answer, Miss Jalapeno?"

"Yes, I would. An American Dream vagina is like a magnet. It is a magnet that draws money, designer clothes, Harry Winston Jewelry, GT Bentley's, Mansions and off-shore bank accounts in your own name. Did I mention minks and furs? I didn't think so. Jen, where you only have that 'pop' I have the 'Pop, Smack, Crackle, and Fire' Vagina."

"I don't mean to interrupt," Zola says, "but I have that 'smack, crackle, and pop' and I don't have half of the things you have."

Jalapeno says, "You got to have that 'Fire Vagina'."

"Bessie immediately says, "The last time my vagina was on fire I had Gonorrhea."

"I'm not talking about that kind of fire. I'm talking about the type of fire that sets a man's heart and soul on fire. I'm sure some of you may think I'm nothing but a gold digger, but I'm not. I found the secret to being an American Dream Successful Vagina,"

"What is the secret?" Jen asked.

"Listen," Jalapeno says, "The less you open your legs to a man, the more you will achieve. The harder I play to get, the more I get from a man. I have made myself a 'Challenger'. I am a challenge to the average man. You also need to understand where I come from, which is Brazil. There are millions of beautiful women just like me, and so we're in serious competition with one another, when we get down with a man, especially a man that has something to offer, we get down all the way! Remember Halle Berry and her ex-husband Eric Benet? Look at her and her baby's father. Well, Halle is said to be one of the most beautiful women that ever lived. Yet her ex-husband went out and had sex with multiple women, beauty is not the only factor in keeping a man. We Latin American Women are the American Dream Vagina. No offense to you ladies. I'm just keeping it real."

"You're no different than the rest of us," said Pam.

Jalapeno asked Pam, "Can you make your vagina speak Spanish and English at the same time?"

"You or any other woman can't make their vagina speak English or Spanish," said Pam.

"Wanna bet me?" Jalapeno asked Pam.

"This is only my opinion. I'm not a psychologist or a psychic. I'm just a man trying to help the female population realize their true worth. A woman's beauty is only her introduction. If I walked into a Bentley Dealership and I see a brand new white 2009 Flying Spur Bentley on the showroom floor, the first word that would come out of my mouth is, 'wow'" and that's the same word a man usually says when he sees a beautiful woman with a nice body. After seeing the Bentley, I would then asked the salesman to let me sit inside of the Bentley to see how it feels. The next three words would be, 'this feels good.' Those same three words are used when a man is having sex with you. I would then ask the salesman to lift the hood up so that I could see what type of engine it had and when I see that there's no engine underneath the hood, the next two words would be, 'I'll pass.' Once again the same words that most men would say after knowing she has nothing else to offer him." I answered.

It was so quiet in the room you could hear a pen drop until Tameika decided to speak.

Tameika fought back tears as she embraced me around the neck. All of the ladies in the room gathered around me. Some shook my hand while others hugged me.

Tameika asked me to escort her to her car. We walked to the car; I looked at her and said, "You take care of yourself."

I turned and started to walk toward my car.

Tameika shouted out, getting my attention. "I'm not a bad person, John."

I turned around and walked back towards her.

She then said "I've been through a lot starting from a very early age. Growing up with no father and a part-time mother made it hard for me. Every boyfriend I've had left me shortly after we had sex. I can't recall one of them staying in my life for more than 30 days. All my life men have dogged me making me feel less than a woman. Then you come along telling me that I'm worth more than men think. You made me feel as though I was worth something. I needed to hear what you had to say and I'm glad that you chose to write this book. In three days I will be twenty-two years old and, I have had sex with at least 30 men. I started having sex at the age of thirteen."

"Wait a minute. Did you say three or three zero?"

"You heard me, Three, zero. I used to think the sooner you give a man some the sooner they would fall in love. I was just lonely looking for love like any other teenage girl, looking for love in all in the wrong places. I turned to other men to fill that void. When I was fourteen I had sex with a man seventy-five years old. He treated me like his daughter," said Tameika as she started to cry.

I held Tameika as she laid her head on my shoulder and cried like a baby.

"Don't cry, Tameika, all of that is behind you now, This is a new day and stop expecting more than you're able to give yourself. Relationships are like bank accounts, because you only get out what you put in. When you decide to start a relationship with a man, make sure that you're able to trust him. Some men will be your friend only when it is convenient for them, but they won't stand by you in times of trouble. I'm sharing wisdom with you, embrace it and it will bring you peace. Make sure he is willing to love you the way you deserved to be loved."

Tameika asked me "Why aren't you married?"

"Because, unlike other men, I refuse to compromise and accept less than what would make me totally happy. I don't want to be half happy."

"What will make you totally happy, if you don't mind me asking?"

"I need a woman that has a full glass of love. It makes it impossible for someone to give you love when their love glass is empty. I need a woman that's not afraid to love and give one hundred and ten percent of herself instead of fifty percent. Don't tell me how much you love me, show me. Action speaks louder than words; and last, I need a friend; a loyal friend is like good medicine when you're sick. This is one of the main reasons why so many relationships don't work.

"What do you mean?"

"It's hard for anyone that was once in love with someone to be friends after a relationship has ended. The key to a successful and healthy relationship is to establish a friendship first and then 'try' to have a sexual relationship, and in the event that relationship doesn't work out, then the two of you could return back to being friends. A true friendship is the real foundation to everything. Remember the three little pigs? One piggy built his house out of sand and the wolf blew his house down. The second little piggy built his house out of straw and the wolf blew his house down, but the third little piggy builds his house out of bricks and the wolf was unable to blow his house down. Build your relationship out of bricks, Tameika.

"That makes so much sense." Tameika replied.

"Remember, a vagina is a terrible thing to waste."

"You mean 'a mind' is a terrible thing to waste?" Tameika attempted to correct me.

"In your case, it's the vagina, honey, and this is my final conclusion after talking to you. Due to the lack of attention you experienced as a child from your father or your mother, you attempted to seek attention elsewhere so you started to dress as though you were a grown woman like most young girls do to attract attention from boys. When you discovered that the majority of boys and men love sex, you decided to trade in your mother's over-size dress and shoes and use what you have between your legs to generate the attention you thought you needed. Take yourself back to your early childhood years, and think about the first time you felt the need for love and attention and how that feeling made you feel. Now you need to realize that you are not going to find fulfillment on the outside until you have peace within." I turned around and headed toward my car. Tameika stood there in the parking lot with her arms crossed, watching me walk to the car. Just before I got out of her sight she yelled out.

"Good night, John Boy!"

I heard Tameika call me by my nickname, so I turned around to question her before she left. "What did you call me?" I asked her.

"I said good night, John Boy."

"How did you know my nickname was John Boy?" I asked.

"You dated my mom twenty three years ago."

"You weren't even born twenty three years ago. How would you know what I look like? I asked.

"I had seen pictures of you and my mom together. I never forget a face." Tameika answered.

"What's your mother's last name?"

"Brumfield."

"What is your last name?"

"Watts."

"Watts?" I repeated.

"Watts, My first name is Tameika but my friends call me Meiko. When I first laid eyes on you in that dark room when you were conducting your book interview I knew in my heart, you were my Father."

"Can't be."

"Why?"

"Because your mother asked me for five hundred dollars so she could pay for an abortion."

"She told me the story."

We stayed in that parking lot talking for about an hour or so. As we were talking I thought to myself 'wow, what a way to find out that you have a daughter, almost 22 years later.' We hugged one another and I watched Tameika as she drove out of the parking lot.

I arrived home shortly after 2:00 am. I could not stop thinking about what happened, and how I went to that club to interview a group of young ladies and how this night changed not only my life, but also several others lives as well. Meeting my daughter for the first time was definitely a shocker for me.

I was overwhelmed as I sat at my computer and begin to document the entire episode from the nightclub. I transferred the data onto my book file, and completed this chapter.

What I found a little disturbing was how so many women had a different prospective when it came to their personal belief about what constitutes an American Dream vagina. So, what really makes up an American Dream Vagina? The different opinions that these eleven women felt made the America Dream Vagina tells me that all women feel differently and they each have an understanding. I also believe it's the person on the receiving end that can only determine if the woman he's with is in fact an American Dream Vagina. Like any other woman with moral standards, self-esteem, and respect for oneself plus they are beautiful, feel that they have the American Dream vagina without being told by a man. They say beauty is only skin deep, when in fact, that may be true, however, many men tend to judge beautify from the outside in. It's hard to see beauty in the inside of a woman, but I do believe that true beauty can reflect from the inside to the outside of her.

For many years America has made young girls and women believe that beauty is light skin with long hair, and a thin physique. Contrary to popular belief, this is not so. I have seen women with dark skin, short hair, hair weaves, and some of them are thick . . . very thick, and they are BEAUTIFUL as well. So, my question is. "Who's right," when it comes down to true beauty? We put so much emphasis on looks that we lose focus of what is true inner beauty. Would looks matter if everyone were blind? Of course not, actually, someone who's beautiful can give you an illusion that she's the one. She's the one you want to marry, the one you would like to bare your children, and the one you can take out and show her off. Women need to stop thinking that because of their outer beauty, everything they need, want and desire should be given to them. I remember my mother saying to my five sisters one day; "Beauty and good looks don't pay the bills."

To all of those good-looking females, you know who you are, the ones with the smooth complexion and nice bodies. Stop using your looks to catch a man, because one day those same looks will disappear and your body will become soft and some cases winkle, your face will sag, and you're not going to be able to move as fast as you're able to move today. Start using your mind, your education, knowledge and wisdom to capture the man you wish to have in your life.

Remember, real love will find you when you least expect it. Looking for love will only cause you to pick up something along the way that you can't get rid of. Be yourself, and I guarantee you that love will find you. Of course, you must be able to recognize love when it comes.

You should also be familiar with the levels of love so when it comes your way you know it. There are seven levels of love, not one or two, but seven. Some will say, "Love is Love," Which represents one love, while many might say; "There's love and being in love," which represents two loves. Only when you know love is when love will find you and remember; Love isn't something you can see. Love is something you feel. Compare love with the wind. Can you see the wind, of course not, but you can feel it. That's true and real love. This is when a woman can become that American Dream Vagina to her American Dream Husband.

As I reclined in my chair, I closed my tired eyes for a moment and I started to pray to myself. "I hope that some girl or woman will read this book, and realize their true worth, and change their life from bad to good. I dedicate this chapter to all the Tameika's in the world who have yet to find their hidden value, Amen."

Chapter Twenty-Five

Gay & Lesbian V Power

Not long ago it was a known fact, if a man was successful in catching a woman, he had the magic touch or the "P-Power," but today those same facts are no longer true. We all know that society has changed. The seemingly real ultimate power is the relationship between Gays and Lesbians. To see two females walking down the street holding hands and kissing one another has become an eye opener for many. Years ago gays and lesbians were afraid to come out of the closet; today they are meeting us at the front door. Being gay or a lesbian is like being black in the 70's, "Say it loud. I'm black and I'm proud." Now there's a new ring-tone, "Say it loud, I'm gay and I'm proud."

I find it amazing that one vagina can be involved with another vagina. I heard that usually when a woman dates another woman it's because they have certain chemistry between them. For a woman to be attracted to another woman, the desire and want must already be present. The rumor is: the average gay woman may not come on to a heterosexual woman, and that lesbians are women that find themselves attracted to another female without actually being gay. Most things in life are usually choices that we make, and when a woman decides to become a lesbian, that is a choice she makes for herself, but on the other hand, a gay woman usually doesn't have that same choice because they are born this way, which makes it difficult to change even when some of them have attempted to change the way they are.

For a long time we have heard that "Opposites Attract" and that opposite works together. For example: Negative and positive, wrong and right, day and night, happiness and sadness, rich and poor, on and off, man and woman, you get the point. So, if any of this holds any truth, then how can the same (female and female), attract one another? Many people feel attracted to people of the same sex, and wonder whether this means that they are gay. For many people these feelings can be intense and alienating. People who are attracted to people of the same sex are usually gay, and they have same sex relationships.

Some people are bisexual and are attracted to men, women, and have relationships with both. Some people are not attracted to anyone, and wonder if this is a sign of homosexuality. Often their uncertainties are revealed with time.

Believing that a lesbian woman can be identified by the way she looks, walks and talk's is a form of pre-judging. Nowadays, the term "lesbian" is used as an expression to homosexual women and this term is derived from Lesbos. The name of the Greek island on which the lesbian poet Sappho lived in antiquity; in the past, homosexual women have been called 'Sapphics' (again after Sappho).

It is believed that many females are born gay, which has been reported to be true through scientific research. Of course being gay isn't the same as being a Lesbian. For years it was assumed that both were the same; lack of knowledge, 'which is something that most individuals suffer from,' is why millions of people on this planet don't understand Gay life and their behavior.

—

There is a difference between the two; this is why there are so many young girls participating in the life of "Lesbianism." Being a lesbian isn't something that you have to be born with, in today's society, the younger generation is turning the act of being lesbian into a New Fad or Trend. Young girls are becoming fascinated with the idea of being in love with their middle school girlfriend or in some cases, their elementary school girlfriend. For years when two women were seen on the dance floor together it was thought of as a form of lesbianism, but this is not true. Some women dance together simply because they don't feel like dancing with any of the men that are around.

I suppose the old cliché does have some truth to it; "Birds of a feather, flock together," I say this because last week, I drove my second to the youngest daughter, Jonice and her favorite cousin down to Venice Beach, and while walking the board-walk I noticed my daughter holding her cousin's right arm as they were walking. So, being the curious father that I am, and a writer of women, relationships, love, control and power, I asked my daughter that old silly question.

"Hey Jonice, when a woman holds hands with another woman, or wraps her arm around another woman's arm while they are walking down the street in public, what does that mean?"

She replied, "It just means you love that person. It has nothing to do with what you're thinking."

"I'm just asking."

"I'm not gay or a lesbian, Daddy. I like boys."

Seconds later, a young boy walked over to my daughter, and asked for her number. Of course she stood there in front of me, and gave him the number while smiling from ear-to-ear.

I shared this story about my daughter and me because again, I allowed my mind to take me into a negative territory when in fact there was nothing wrong. The majority of us are the same. We see things, and we immediately pass judgment. If it doesn't look right we ask questions, if it looks out of place, we ask questions, if it looks different, we're going to ask questions, and if we feel a certain way about something, believe me, we're going to ask a million and one questions. Of course I didn't have a million and one questions for my daughter; I was just being a Dad.

Is it true that a woman knows what another woman needs, wants, and desires?

Is it true that women know what turns another woman on, or off which is why they know what to do to keep her turned on?

Do most women turn to another woman after experiencing a failed marriage or relationship with a man?

Or is it just out of curiosity and wanting to fit in to what is cool to others? It really doesn't matter what drew one woman to another. My point is there are more and more women engaging in same-sex relationships than ever before. Our new generation is standing at the front door, wearing a t-shirt that said; "I'm proud to be Gay", or, "Lesbianism is my choice."

We really do live in a country where there's freedom of speech, and the freedom to express who you are or who you wish to become.

Just the other day I was introduced to a young woman named Brenda, she and I agreed to meet at a nearby fast food restaurant for an interview. Brenda is in her mid thirties, with four children and she lives in a home with her same-sex partner.

"As I stated to you on the phone last night that I am writing a book and the title is 'Power of the Vagina,' I am working on a chapter entitled 'Gay and Lesbian 'V' Power.' I wanted to meet with you to talk about your sexual preference. Now you mentioned to me over the phone that you no longer date men, and now have a woman in your life."

"That is correct, and she makes me so happy. If I had known that a same-sex relationship had this much to offer, I would have chosen a woman over a man a long time ago."

"What can a woman offer that a man can't?" I asked.

"Everything, the woman I'm with doesn't argue with me. She doesn't beat me. She makes sure I'm okay and she knows how to love me."

"What was the breaking point to cause you to go from a man to a woman?" I asked.

Brenda stared at me for a minute in silence before saying a word, and then tears started to run down the side of her face. I walked over to the cashier's window and asked for some napkins. I returned where Brenda was sitting, and handed her the napkins to dry her eyes.

"Thank you. I didn't mean to cry, I'm sorry. I feel so embarrassed, plus I don't even know you."

"It's okay let me re-phase my question. Was it the woman that made you switch, or was it the beating from the man?"

"It was the beating, for the past fourteen years I have endured name-calling, and I mean he would call me every name in the book. On Fridays, I was fifty "Bitches", on Saturday, I was a hundred "Motha-F#@kas", and on Sunday, I was a hundred and twenty-five "Motha F#@kin Bitches." Tuesday thru Thursday I was his punching bag. He has given me at least a half of dozen black eyes, my ribs have been broken twice, and my jaw has been dislocated several times as well. It comes to a point in one's life when you have to take a stand and say to yourself, enough is enough."

"So, it wasn't the woman?"

"No, not at first, I wasn't born gay and I have never thought about becoming a lesbian. It was something that just happened. She was my best friend for many years and one day she visited me at the hospital. I was there because of a dislocated shoulder, and she sat beside me held my hand, and looked me dead in my eyes and said to me, "If you don't leave your baby daddy, he's going to kill you. You and the kids can come and stay with me. I'll take care of you." Then tears started to roll down her face.

I just nodded my head.

"A few days later I was discharged from the hospital, I went back to the house while my man was at work. I moved everything out of that house into her place. As each day went by, I found myself lonely for the touch of a man. One night, Liz, that's her name, and I were sitting around the house having some drinks. Well, one thing led to another, and before I knew it, I was spread across her queen size bed butt naked. From that night on we became lovers, and for the first time in my adult life, I felt the love from a human being. I never knew what love was; I never knew what it felt like until I met her."

"So, does this mean that you're now gay or a lesbian?" I asked.

"It makes me a lesbian because I wasn't born this way, and I still have feelings for men and one day I might find myself with another man. Who knows, but for now I like the way she makes me feel."

"I can't say that I truly understand, but I understand, if that makes any sense."

"A Lesbian is a woman who decided to be with another woman and these types of women are not born gay?" I asked.

"Correct. Look at me. I still have feelings for men." Brenda replied as she smiled at me.

"So, it's a life style for gay women, and a fad or trend for most lesbians?"

"I suppose you can say that, but let's not forget about the "Butch" woman."

"Isn't gay and butch the same?" I asked.

"No, A gay woman usually keeps her femininity, but a butch, is a woman that wants to be a man. They are the ones who wear men clothes, and shoes. Butch women usually wear their hair cut short to look more like a boy or man. They walk, talk and act like a man," Brenda answered.

"So, there are gays, lesbians and butches?"

"Yes, but the butches usually prefer people to call them "Studs." You rarely hear the word Butch."

"So, if I asked you do you believe that gay women, lesbians and studs have the "V" power? What would be your final answer?"

"Yes most definitely."

If that's true, why are there so many young women today falling for another woman, when they could simply use their power and catch a man? Everywhere I go I see teenage girls hugged up with one another. Just the other day, I saw two teenage girls kissing at the bus stop.

For years, if you were gay or a lesbian, you would keep your sexual preferences behind closed doors, and not in public. The Jerry Springer shows, and other shows, like his television show, have become more and more popular and accepted. It's now a part of our society and a lot of young females today are merely confused. How could a young girl ten years old wake up one morning, go to school and come home a lesbian? It's a fad, it's a trend. Some young women think it's cute to walk down the street holding hands, and hugging another woman. Most of these girls today have no idea what they're doing. They're playing "Monkey see, Monkey do."

I thanked Brenda for taking the time to speak to me. I headed back to my car and left.

We as a society should not pre-judge or judge one's sexual preference. Of course, most people would probably like to see a world that follows moral biblical standards, where men married women and women married men, however, society is changing. There are still countries that don't allow any type of gay or lesbian acts, but even then, one still doesn't know if it exists or not because, what's done in the dark stays in the dark when you're not accepted for who you wish to become, while living your life.

I believe whatever makes you happy and brings peace into your life is where you should be and spend your time. The above story is typical of many women that have experienced an abusive relationship with a man. I can understand how someone can say to themselves, "Enough is enough," and seek love and peace-of-mind elsewhere. This is not to say that all abusive relationships end up in lesbian relationships. Today, more and more young women are participating in lesbian acts. Some might say that these young women are lost and some may say these young women are just confused. Rather they are lost or confused they should know what they are really involved in because they may end up hurting the other person who's involved.

Where there is a woman, there is V power. Where there are female, gays, and lesbians, there is super V power.

Chapter Twenty-Six

Teenage V's Gone Wild

Have teenage females gone wild? After watching an episode of girls gone wild and talking to a dozen of wild teenage girls, I felt the need to write a chapter about young females with wild vaginas. One of my friends told me that her 13 year old son went to a graduation party. Apparently the party was not supervised because her son told her that two of the girls (ages 11) took turns giving him a lap dance with oral sex to follow. Here is a story about a group of teenage girls that believe, being off the hook and having an attitude like they don't give a damn is the best way to live their lives.

Back in the late 70's and early 80's teen-age girls looked like and carried themselves like they were teenagers. Today, many teen-age girls look and act like adult women. Some might even say the way young girls dress these days, displaying everything they have, is a sign of not giving a damn about themselves, but it goes much further than that. I believe this generation of teen-age females, and I'm speaking of the teen-age girls that fit this profile, have taken life into their own hands and out of the hands of their parents. Hanging out until five o' clock in the morning is only part of being a teen-age girl gone wild. Drugs of the new millennium, such as, Meth, Cough Syrup, and Ecstasy are some of the contributing drugs that are turning our teen-age girls out.

Parents how do you know if your teenage daughter has gone wild? How is she doing in school? Are her grades slipping? Is she cutting class? Have you suddenly appeared at her school, only to find out that the clothes she has on are ones that she did not leave home in, and that you have never seen before? Is she suddenly lying about where she is and who she is with? Does she have friends that you know nothing about? Has her behavior dramatically changed for the worst?

Teen pregnancy and suicide have risen in the past ten years. In this chapter a group of six teen-age girls sit around sharing their wild stories with one another.

"G-I-R-L, last night I came up on seventy-nine dollars by having sex with five guys. I was walking home from this party and before I could get home, I was approached like ten times. After the fifth guy, my poor little vagina was worn out," Kelli says.

Dottie says, "Last night I had sex with a drug dealer in exchange for some of that good ass Cush."

"I've been high all night long off that ecstasy. I haven't been home in like three whole days. I have no idea how many men I slept with. All I can remember is, being on my back and my boyfriend climbing on top of me, but I recall him telling his home boys about how good my stuff was and that it's the bomb," Said Lynnette.

"Girl you know you need to put on some more clothes before we go out," Kelli said to Joyce.

Joyce shouted out, "Put on more clothes. Are you crazy? If you don't show what you got to men, they will find it somewhere else. There is an orgy party tonight not far from my parent's house. They have them every other Friday. I heard the parties are cool and off the hook."

"I love orgies. Everything goes, which is definitely up my alley." Dottie said.

"Well," says Lynnette, "I need to get home to change clothes. I have had on the same undies for six days."

"Girl, take them panties off, jump in the shower and do you. Wild girls don't wear panties anyway," Kelli says.

They laugh and hi-five one another.

These teen-age girls might believe that they are having the time of their life, however, I think it is sad. Some of the females in generation X have no idea what it feels like to be a decent teenager who participates in normal activities that teenage girls used to do back in my day. I remember being a teenager sat on the side of the curb and watched teenage girls play, "Hop Scotch," "Tether ball," "House," "Jacks," and sometimes just sitting around conversing with their teenage girlfriends. I would rarely see a teenage girl wearing a dress or skirt above her knee, and seeing a young female with a tattoo was un-heard of.

The difference between the teenage girls in my day and some of teenage girls today is three simple things; Morals, integrity, and self-respect. Even though the definition was rarely shared with the teenage girls back in my day, you knew if it was taught within their households because of their actions. I'm almost a hundred percent sure if you walked up to an average wild teenage girl between the ages of 13 to19 she probably wouldn't know the definition of morals, integrity, or self-respect. Until one learns the true meaning of these three words, their lives will never change for the good, it will only get worse.

Teenage vaginas gone wild actually means teens between the ages of 13 to 19 having sex with boys and often grown men. They even have sex with girls of their own ages. To be wild is a form of not thinking about what is being done to you, or of the act in which it is performed. Passionately kissing another girl as if you are kissing a boy is getting to be the norm in our society, and because more and more teenage girls are behaving this way, it's almost like some new trend. Being wild is the new cool, except being too cool sometimes comes with price.

It has been reported that teenage girls have an eight-five percent chance of becoming pregnant within twelve months when they practice un-protected sex. One out of every five teenage girl is infected with the HIV virus, and three out of ten are infected with herpes. Even though these statistics are advertised daily on television and magazines, wild teenage girls are constantly ignoring the warning signs. To be a wild teenage girl is actually showing how you are not cultivated and you are acting in an uncivilized manner. Wild teens are out of control when they are not guided by their parents, teachers, or any positive influences. Wild teenage girls are definitely undisciplined, unruly, rowdy, and disorderly and they are usually in pursuit of self-pleasure. It's one thing to get dressed and go out to a wild party one night, but these teenage girls are becoming the party, and the party is being played in their heads every single day and night.

In today's elementary, middle, and high schools, girlfriends are becoming the new boyfriends. It appears that a lot of young and some adult females are playing the same games that boys and men play. When a man plays or cheats on his girlfriend or wife he is called a "Dog?" Well, young and some adult females are starting to play the same "Dog Game" on boys and men today. Where a man is called a "Dog," women are being called "Wild."

I hope that these teenage females come to the realization that there is more to life than parties, drinking, drugs, and sex.

This chapter is about teenage vaginas gone wild, it is not meant for young females, who do not behave in this manor, to admire this type of conduct. It is meant to change the behavior of those who carry on this way and those who have no clue. This type of lifestyle can only lead them to a life of moral destruction.

To hear about what you're doing is one thing, but to actually be able to see or read about it and to recognize that this is how you conduct yourself is another. Will this chapter and my written words change the minds of these teenage girls? Maybe; however, I believe it will give them something to think about and it will get them to take a look in the mirror, but before this can happen, I believe the definition should be exposed to these wild teenage girls. So, here are the definitions of morals, integrity and self-respect:

Morals: Concerned with the principles of right and wrong behavior and the goodness or badness of human character: adhering to the code of interpersonal behavior that is considering right or acceptable in a particular society: manifesting high principles for proper conduct: examining the nature of ethics and the foundation of good and bad character and conduct: while moral refers to generally accepted standards of goodness and rightness in character ad conduct—especially sexual conduct (*the moral values she's learned from her mother, or other positive female role models*).

Integrity: The quality of being honest and having moral principles; moral uprightness: *she is known to be a woman of integrity.* The state of being whole and undivided: internal consistency of lack of corruption: the condition of being unified, unimpaired, or sound in construction: honor, ethics, moral, virtuous, and decent.

Self-respect: Pride and confident in self is a feeling that one is behaving with honor and dignity.

So let's keep these wild females in our thoughts, and our prayers and hope this doesn't happen to our daughters.

Chapter Twenty-Seven

Is Anyone Immune to the V?

The answer is no. Majority of straight men enjoys it. Some gay men wish they had one and lesbians had to have two of them.

Some straight men have become obsessed with the vagina and they will do almost anything for it: Sell drugs, commit a crime, steal, rob, rape and even kill. Have you ever asked yourself, why do men dress up in expensive clothing and drive around in expensive cars? It's all for you ladies, believe it or not. The average man can throw on a pair of blue jeans, a t-shirt, and a pair of tennis shoes and be on his way. We believe that dressing up and driving the latest expensive car will get the attention of women, which is why some men do it. This is not the case for all men. Some men believe they have the gift-of-gab, so this wouldn't apply to them or to the men that need these possessions to increase their self-confidence. Now, picture if there were no women in the world. Would a $3,000 suit, $1,500 pair of shoes, and a car that cost over $100,000 matter?

Of course not, the things some straight men do is all for you ladies.

I also would like to address the word "Steal and Rob." These two words could play a part if a man is addicted to drugs. He would go out and steal and rob to support his drug habit, but there is an exception where a man would go out and steal and rob and use the money to purchase some of the same things I mentioned earlier, just to impress the ladies.

When we look back on the history of the vagina, it has been through more trauma than any other body part. It has been stretched, slapped, bitten, scratched, pulled, abused, injured, cloned, mistreated, hospitalized, cut, scoped, raped, damaged, torn apart, played with and talked about and yet it still comes in first place.

As I stated in the title, "Is Anyone Immune to The Vagina" the answer remains "No." There's isn't anyone in the world that is immune to the V. Every boy, girl, man and woman are susceptible to the vagina which is why . . .

"The Oscar for best performance goes to the . . . Vagina"

Chapter Twenty-Eight

Who Really Has the Power?

Men or Women?

Approximately one hundred men and one hundred women were asked the same question regarding V power. Thirty-eight comments were randomly selected for this chapter. I learned a lot and I'm sure so did the ones that had no idea what V power meant. It was surprising to find out that plenty of men agreed that women held the power. I had no idea what I was getting myself into when I set out to get people's opinion about who really has the power, men or women. As much as I attempted to convince a few men that women hold the power. Some became a little disturbed and an argument almost erupted. Some men may not accept the fact that women hold the power.

Here is a list of the top thirty comments from both men and women and their opinion of who they think holds the power and why.

Brenda, 51 "You know the women rule. Who was it that got the man to eat the forbidden fruit? THE WOMAN. Who was the weak one who fell for it? THE MAN. Although man is supposed to have the power . . . and some men do and there are others who are still eating the forbidden fruit, if you know what I mean."

Lesley, 45 "The ability to hold a job does not give one dominion over the other. It's naive to think, that the one who has more, is the one that should get all the respect. I think that a man has a lot to offer to a woman and a woman has a lot to offer a man. By having the ability to share that power among one another is when power is truly in force. The benefit of having a mate is so that when two halves come together they make a whole."

Sheila, 48 "I believe it's the woman who has the power and I'm going to tell you why. When the sex is good to a man, there's nothing he won't do for it. He will leave his wife, and children, and walk away from his home. The woman holds the ultimate power because of her ability to cause a man to do what I just mentioned. Look at all of the politicians that have gotten caught up over the past twenty years over the vagina. That alone tells us who has the power. Remember, women don't know they have the power until a man reveals it to them. I rest my case."

Netti, 43 "Women are more powerful today than they were in the past. No more taking the back seat for real women. We can do everything a man can do. We're self-sufficient. We no longer have to depend on a man. Let me rephrase that. We prefer a man sexually, but we don't need a man sexually if you get my point. A man supposes to be our helpmate not a liability to the woman. I have never had a man to put me up on game or enhance me. A successful woman intimidates most men. I'm not in competition with my man or any other man. I am the prize at the end of the day to a man. Real women have a voice. We're speaking up and speaking out."

Phyllis, 51 "Men control 80% of money in the world. Women control 100% of the Pussy. If you could be filthy rich, but you had to give up sex would you still choose being rich? That is my answer."

Paul, 53 "I believe a man has power over some things. Men express their power through work and the daily challenges we face from just being men. Most women with power usually don't have to do anything, except be a lady. I do feel that a woman has that hidden power, that soft subtle power that's usually not expressed in public places. Her power is usually not exposed. What I have come to learn is. Most women have power with that seductive look, but only a real man would recognize that. We men have an ego. Men know it's about the woman. That is why we get up every day and go out there and make things happen. It's for the woman. If you read the book *48 Laws of Power* you will find that wars were fought and lost over a woman."

Latanya, 38 "Some men will think they have the power because of money and I understand. Money does hold the power. So, when you ask me that question, who really has the power. It's not a person, its money. I have met men that don't give a damn about the vagina. Most men have a high sex drive, which is why they put the vagina over everything. There are some men that can't work because they're hooked on it. I am aware that money can't buy happiness, but it can buy you temporary happiness. With the brain, one can manipulate another person and never have sex. As a woman, I just think its money that holds the power and not the vagina."

E.T., 46 "Women hold the power, bottom line. Men cannot live on bread alone, we need the woman. We fall short for sex. If a man cheats on his woman and she finds out, she's hurt, but we don't let it affect us. On the other hand, if that same woman goes out and cheats on a man we would want to kill somebody. Men are tricks and they're weak. Adam fell short because of Eve. A man can hear a rumor about a woman and want to have a piece of her because of what he has heard. For example, if we hear that a woman has some good vagina. Nine-out-of-ten in our mind, we need to have some of that. That's power. I admit that I'm weak for the V and I can't lie about it. After doing time in the pen, a man tends to want more than average. Trying to play catch up, I have allowed women in the street to be my downfall. I need to be thankful for my wife, but instead I'm letting other things take priority over my thoughts. Women got the power. Put that in your book."

Victoria, 50 "The man is supposed to have the power over the woman according to the bible, but not all men exercise that power. When a man becomes addicted to sex the woman holds the power due to his addiction. The V was a gift from God to all women from birth. Women need to take time out for self and learn about their own power. Do you guys know that the woman can do more with the V than a man with his P? A woman can carry a child for months, she can give birth to a human being, and she can use it to please a man. As little girls growing up our mothers told us to say no to sex. Indirectly she was telling us to wait for marriage, and that we had the power. Some men will say that they can satisfy themselves, and that may be true to a certain extent, however, it's nothing like being satisfied by a woman. Take a man fifteen years older than a woman. His experience, self-wisdom and age gap will make him feel as if he has power. The vagina only has the power if the woman knows the power it possesses. It's all in the mind, so therefore the woman has the POWER!!!"

Gayle, 52 "I believe it's the woman because we are protectors, nurturers, and advisors. Women wear a lot of hats, and most of the time we are the driving force in the relationship. We give support to our companion; we encourage them in their endeavors. Real women do not have a problem with standing beside their companion as well behind them. A woman of power knows how to use her God given power she is gentle, graceful, intelligent, a good listener and God fearing. She has love for herself and knows who she is, she is confident, and honest, she also learns from her mistakes. Some women do not realize the power that has been given to them and that is sad because it is a gift that they have not taken the time to unwrap and embrace."

Shontel, 39 "Both the man and the woman has the power. I say that because, the man is supposed to be the strong one in a male figure and do for his woman, which sometimes that can become a false illusion to a woman. I also feel that a woman has the power because of her place as a woman, and when she's in a relationship with a man. The V needs the P and the P compliments the V. I have witnessed men having the power, and women having the power over men. I can't say it's the man and I won't say it's the woman."

Pam, 51 "Women have always held the power; she has what a man wants and needs simultaneously. A man has both emotional and physical needs. Of course, the physical outweighs emotional needs. The V can be an addiction if a man isn't careful. Take a woman that is a home-wrecker, she will creep up under your husband or man and be willing to surrender all of herself on demand. More women need to get to know themselves and in doing so they will find their power through confidence, which will help a woman to execute her game. A man's power is limited. A man with power is because of a woman that doesn't know she has the power."

Shamira, 24 "A man that dates young stupid girls will always have the power over them because they know no better, but if he dates a smart intelligent girl, she will end up having the power. If a woman can get the man to chase her, she holds the power. Look at the older women that are out here chasing these young boys in exchange for money. Who holds the power? It isn't the boys. It's the "Cougar" (older woman that have sex with younger men). It places the power into her hands, she has the money, she makes the date for where, when, time and the location. The boy is there to service the woman that is his only purpose. As for as prostitutes, they definitely don't hold any power regardless, if they stood on street corners or used the Internet for sex entertainment. They're powerless."

JoAnn, 55 "Of course it's the woman; she has the power to make things what it becomes. It's what she says or not says. She controls her relationship.

This comes with age and experience. The average woman can break or make a man. She can mode the man. She can get the man to do whatever it is she needs done. Now, don't get me wrong, sex plays a big part and age plays a part. Take a young woman age 25; she's not going to have any idea where her power lies. It isn't until a woman is in her late forties or early fifties before she discovers her real power. I may sound a little mean for saying this, but it is what it is. A young woman under 25 is just a vagina even though to me the vagina is powerful, period."

Juan, 47 "My dick is worth millions of dollars and I've never been pussy whooped, but I have been in love before. I love pussy, but I love myself more. I don't pay a woman's bills just to lay with them, but I will pay a bill or two for love. What women don't know about me is. When I give, I give from the kindness of my heart. I don't believe in "Trickalydis," (which means giving your money to women for exchange of sex). When I spend time with a woman after my initial interview with her I am planning on settling down with that woman. I'm too old to play games. A woman's cover looks good in the beginning. Sex to me is the icing on the cake, but I can also eat the cake without the icing. At 50, I will take intellect over sex all day. She also needs to be a woman of God, and willing to go through the good and bad with me. Remember, God made man first."

L.C., 52 "The man is supposed to be the head and hold the power, but today with all of these 'Pussy-Like-Men' walking around faking wanting to be men, the women now holds the power."

Ant, 39 "Men have the power. God's natural order for man is to rule over women, and children. Since then woman have come into the power. Women were put on earth to help and aid her man. I follow God's order it's my way or no way. All women have an opinion, but we all know it's the Kings who rule the Queens. The ultimate decision falls on the man. There are women leaders, but it isn't her natural position. And far as a woman ever becoming the President of the United States of America, it will never happen."

Ms. Tagg, 47 "Women because we are the foundation we keep everything together. We have that power. The reason I feel this way is because I watched my mama over the years. How she kept the family together, the household and so on. However, since she passed away, everything seems to have fallen apart. As I am going through my life right now, I'm experiencing what and how my mama kept everything together. Women, we are the foundation.

Bruce, 46 "I believe it's the individual who has the power. The power is knowledge. Once you become too old to have sex, then would the vagina matter? Hell no. If a man could talk a woman into standing on the corner, turn a trick and bring back the money to him. He holds the power. First you get the knowledge, then the money and with those two things anyone can achieve the power. Enough money can buy you all the vagina you want and desire. If a woman has so much power, why is she unsuccessful in getting a gay man to have sex with her?"

Laura, 51 "Women hold the power. The woman has an oil well. All we need to know is how to drill it. My daddy told me that when I was just a little girl. So far, he's right."

Dorion, 20 "Man holds the power. Man determines the path of his household. He also calls the shots in his relationship. The household will fall apart if the man doesn't play his role. This is not to say that women don't hold any power. I just believe that it's the man that holds just a little bit more power than the woman. As far as the bedroom goes, the woman holds all the power."

FranShawn, 33 "A woman who has knowledge of herself holds the power, but if a man acquires the same knowledge as a woman that will cause the two of them to hold the power equally. The lack of knowledge is the separation of power, which means neither man nor woman hold the power. When a woman is in a relationship she has to learn when to exercise her power and when to be submissive."

Burbank, 55 "The woman has the power because there are too many tricks (weak men) that are being tricked by bitches and hoes. Bitches have taken the power from the men. Of course, I'll never let a bitch trick me out of a glass of cold water on a hot summer day; however, I must keep it real with you John. It's the woman that holds the real power and I never thought I would see the day that I would say those words, but hell it's true."

Bryon, 71 "Who really holds the power, hell the woman does. A woman is so bad she makes the man think he has the power. Believe it or not, pussy rules the world. Take these millionaire Ball Players. They think it's their money that caught the woman which in fact. It was the pussy that caught the Ball Players."

Officer, S. Brown, 49 "Men have the power from the beginning of time; God put man to sleep and drew a rib from him to create a woman. Physical strength goes to the man; spiritual strength goes to the woman. Adam was given the command, but he allowed the woman's curiosity to cause him to disobey God's order. An old man once told me when I was a kid. "Look young man, you're the catch, not the woman."

Nechelle, 47 "The man does and the Bible says so, but why should the man be the head? I can think for myself. The majority of women are more responsible than men, when it comes to our households. We also hold the power in the bedroom, because we know all of the tricks. Most times men need help in the bedroom. Here's the one mistake that most men make in the bedroom. He compares his last sexual relation with his new sexual partner. The second reason why I feel as though I have the power is because, after sex. The next day, my man will get up and head to work or get out in those streets and make some kind of money. I never needed a man to validate me; I validate myself as a woman. More women need to have self-esteem and never take second position when it comes down to a man. Have respect for one-self. I can say; all pussy isn't good pussy. Every time I sit down, I'm sitting on a million dollars. That's the power of the V."

The General, A.K.A. Dobbie, 54 "Bitches got the power. Both pimps and suckas know that. A man will kill over a piece of pussy before a bitch would kill over a piece dick. Take majority of men and so-called pimps. When shit hits the fan and things get hard for the average man or pimp. He will break down like a bitch, but while things are all good, he sticks his chest out, and holds his head up as if he's the man with the power. A real man does not get weak in a crisis, and a strong-minded man is a man 24/7. At the end of the day, these types of men are nothing, but a sucka with pimp dialog. The average man my age is kissing bitch's asses just to have a place to lay their head. I still got two old hoes left in my stable and they do their best everyday to bring home some kind of money. Pussy just isn't selling like it use to, I know that. These men out here got girlfriends. Isn't that ugh bitch? As for me, I haven't got no woman and don't need one. What I have seen in this pimp game is pressure will break a sucka, and it's hard to find a stand up man or pimp and this is real talk from a real man.

Robert, 28 "I think it's the woman that holds the power, because she has something that we need. Men seem too weak without a woman. Women are stronger than men. Most men do dumb shit and make stupid decisions. Women think the opposite and they usually think before acting. A woman can find a man much quicker than a man can find a woman. The women out here are materialistic. If a man has money, he becomes the power. Some men know how to manipulate a woman which means he doesn't have to use any money to be in control, making the man powerful. If you can keep a woman laughing, compliment her from time to time, tell her what she wants and needs to hear and make her feel like she's important. One day she, might surrender her power to you, or give you the power to wear sometimes. Without the woman, there can be no children, no life, any future. They simply have the power."

Maurice, 40 "Honesty! Most women have more power than men do. The reason why I say that is because Ninety-nine point nine percent of men will pay a woman for sex before a woman would pay a man for sex. Women are more mental and men are more physical. If a man can get a woman in the mood he can have his way with her, but if he takes her out of the mood, his chance of getting anything that night is over. It's easy to get a woman out of the mood. Believe me. All you have to do is say something silly or stupid, which most men usually do before the night is over. Women can also make a man feel like he has the power. I was raised around a lot of women including my grandmother and her sister, those two were something else. I never met anyone like them. I watched my sisters play men. Another reason why women have the power is because every day, men stay on the hunt for a female."

Erin, 24 "Women hold the power. I was taught that when I was eleven years old by my mom, grandma, and aunts. They all knew they held the power. Women are made to be wanted by men. When a man reaches a certain age, they tend to understand it, but sometimes its way into their fifty's. My power has worth. A man has a "Smidgen" of power, compared to a woman. A woman's sexual activities have nothing to do with power. What makes a woman so powerful is her intellect and inner beauty. The respect level determines how much power you hold and it's not the sex. A woman's comfort can be a sign of power. Power is found. Every woman has the power, but every woman doesn't know how to use it."

Jonice, 16 "In my book, high school boys have the power over high school girls. Most girls are vulnerable. If the boy is cute and says the right words, the girls fall for the guy. Peer pressure also plays a part when it comes to making their decisions. There are a lot of weak girls when it comes down to sex and boys. Just because a boy says: "I love you." Doesn't mean he really does. Boys will lie to get what they want and that is including sex. What's funny is eight out of ten girls do it, just to fit in. I find most girls in L.A., aren't smart compared to other Cities. Girls don't listen to other girls or their parents."

Treasure, 49 "Of course women has the power. Even though we were created through Adam's rib, it was a woman that controlled Adam, not a man. It what's between a woman's legs that allows her the ability to control; any man on earth, but she has to know her power and a lot of women don't know their power. We weren't taught about the power in our homes growing up, many of us don't read the bible, and most women especially younger women are just plain ignorant. Women today only tend to play games with men. If the average woman holds out on a man she can get what she really wants from him. Some women think giving it up quickly wins over the man. It's not just about the vagina. It's about one's intellect among other things. I'm guilty of being a little naive. I gave up my power when I didn't have to. Another thing is you need to know what to do with that power. If men today start acting like real men they could win the power back from the woman or at least share the power. Believe it or not, when a man admires a woman from across the room and later walks over to speak with her. At that moment, she's in the power seat. All decisions are on her. A woman can be cold and calculating when she wants to."

Earl, 36 "The female has more power than the man, but one doesn't work without the other. Females no longer need a man which gives them power. My wife has more power than me. A woman can want a man, but she can hold out. A man will go out and look for something else to screw, and he doesn't have to be in love, hell he doesn't have to know her name. Weakness in a man is a sign of not having any power. The woman is powerful in the bedroom. Back in the day the woman was dependent on the man; those days are so far behind us."

Portia, 48 "I hold the power as long as I have a vagina. My father once told me; "As long as you have a pussy you should never be broke," and I believe it. The power is in the pussy."

David, 48 "Man holds the power. It goes back to ancient time. Before woman it was man. Man should have dominion and power over woman. She only has power in the household. No vagina has absolute power. The vagina was never intended to control a man. It was given to her to bare children, and to please her man. Where there is no male or male figure in the household, there can never be any real power, and this is in no way disrespect toward women. God said; man should love his wife as the Christ loved the church and it also says: Wives submit yourself to your husband. God gave men the power. Man controls the woman."

Lawanda, 45 "Yes the woman has the power without a doubt in my mind. You need to know your worth. Then you have the power. Knowing your true worth is the V power. It's only when a woman doesn't know her worth is when the man takes over the power especially when he knows the power women holds. Most women need a man to validate them and without a man they feel worthless and powerless. I have validated myself. The vagina is the third most important body part on the body coming in third place behind the brain and the heart. God has offered sex to the man as a reward when he's married. A man without maturity can and will be controlled by the vagina but a man with wisdom and has had his share of sex. That becomes his power. Remember, the vagina will eventually get old as women gets older."

Kia, 33 "Men have muscular strength and women have more inner strength for example; when a man is weak the women is able to lift him up using that inner strength. All women have the power, but some are not aware that they have it. There are some women out there who are manipulative and conniving and they use their power for the wrong reasons. Young ladies have the power as well but many of them are unaware of it, because they lack representation in their own home. They have no one to teach them how a lady should conduct herself at all times. In my daughters peer group (ages 14 to 16) some of them allow young boys to control them, because in their mind they believe the boy likes them. If young ladies knew who they were, and the power they have, they would carry themselves in a way that the boys would show them respect. Women do hold the power, but a real woman knows when to be submissive."

Summer, 42 "Men have always had and always will hold the power. Why, because men don't function on emotions women do, which makes us weaker and men stronger."

John Watts, Author, 50 "The reason why I feel as though women hold the power is because a woman has proven to be smart, great organizers, better planners, super mothers, reasonable thinkers and great wives when she is married to the right man. A woman reminds me of the game called Chess. It's the Queen that holds the most power on the board, because she is the most important piece that offers full protection to the King. She keeps him from being 'Check Mated.' Again, her job is to protect. In the game of Chess, if the woman or in this case, the Queen lies down, gets taken or refuses to do her job, her King is open for attacks. What makes men wise is when he has reverence for women, and knows that it is them who hold the ultimate power. I salute every woman on earth, and I pray that you all find your true power."

Chapter Twenty-Nine

Power of Love and Forgiveness

One afternoon I was sitting around the halfway house, and I decided to catch the bus to my mother's house. I borrowed ten dollars for gas; my mother's old 1999 Maxima and headed over to 64th near West Boulevard to visit with my two daughters and my grandchildren whom I had never seen. I knew it was time for us to sit down and talk about some of the things that took place in our lives over the years. I was hoping that the three of us could feel the power of love through forgiveness. I wanted them to know just how much they mean to me. Last but not least, it was time to forgive one another for all of the wrong we caused in each other's lives.

Some prisoners sit around waiting to be released so they can hurry and find themselves a woman to screw, or they look for some good weed to smoke. All I could think about were my daughters, Dominece, Tameika, Jonice and Sidnee forgiving me and putting the past behind them so they could love me the way a father wants to be loved. That would mean the world to me.

When I pulled up in front of this old rundown apartment complex and parked, I wasn't sure if I should get out of the car or sit there. There was a crowd of people hanging out in front of the building. I mean there were at least twenty-five young men, and women drinking, smoking weed and dancing to the music that came from different apartments. After I decided to get out of the car, I made my way to the front gate where approximately six gang bangers were standing in front of a rusty iron gate, which happened to be the only entry into the complex.

"Excuse me," I said to the guys as I stood there waiting for them to clear the way for me to get through.

"What's up, Cuzz?" one of the gangbangers said to me as he stood there with a joint in one hand and an Old English 800 in the other.

"Ain't nothing up," I answered with my hands behind my back waiting to see if they were going to let me through.

They moved to the side just enough to let me by. I made my way through the guys and walked down the walkway looking for apartment number five. My daughter Tameika noticed me and ran to greet me.

"Hi Daddy, I am glad to see you again." She said as she grabbed me around my neck and hugged me as tight as she could. Tears ran down the both of our faces. I held on to Tameika as if I never wanted to let go of her, then I heard someone call my name, then they called my name again. This time the soft female voice came from over Tameika's shoulder.

"Hi Dad," said my oldest daughter, Dominece. The two of us hugged one another.

Tameika grabbed me by the hand and said," Let's go inside, Daddy. Come on Dominece."

One of the young girls from the crowd yelled out. "Who is that Tameika?"

"Mind your own business!" Tameika shouted back at her.

Dominece grabbed my other hand and the three of us headed inside of Tameika's apartment.

Tameika said, "Have a seat, Daddy. I'm sure this is nothing like what you had at your Bel Air Mansion, but it's the best I can do. Can I get you anything to drink: Orange juice, milk, water, or Kool-Aid?"

"What flavor of Kool-Aid do you have?" I asked.

"Red, I mean Cherry, I just made a half of a pitcher last night so it should be sweet and cold."

"Yes, I'll have a glass of Kool-Aid with some ice."

"Dominece, you want a cup of Kool-Aid?" Tameika asked.

"Sure, I'll have a cup."

I sat back, and admired my grandkids as they played with their toys. It kind of reminded me of when I was a little boy playing with my hot wheel cars and my G.I Joe army men. Not only am I a proud father. I have something else to be proud of; Dominece has two sons and was expecting her third child and Tameika has a son and daughter.

Tamieka broke the silence by asking, "So, Daddy, are you happy to be home?"

"Happy isn't the word. I've been gone nine years."

"That's a long time Dad, actually too long. Dominece said when you left I was 14, Jonice was 7, Tameika was 13, and Sidnee was 5. Was it hard in there, Dad?"

"No, I spent all my time working, typing, and exercising, and I stayed away from the B.S. There were only a few guys who I hung out with."

Tameika asked "Did you have to fight anybody in there."

"No fights, being 6'4" and weighing close to 240 pounds gave me a little advantage," I answered as we laughed.

"I can't speak for Dominece, Daddy, but as for me not visiting you I never knew where you were. I also knew you didn't know you had another daughter because of what you were told a long time ago. I also want you to know that I thought about you all of the time. I used to stare at your pictures my mom had in her photo album," Tameika said as she started to tear up.

"Don't cry, baby. It's all good and I don't blame you," I said to Tameika as I reached over and held her.

"I'm sorry, too, Dad. I didn't get a chance to talk to you about me not coming to visit you at Grandma's the other night. As you could tell, I was pretty upset with my boyfriend AJ, plus I didn't have a car to come visit. Believe it or not, after you left my whole life changed. I felt like the whole world had crumbled down on top of me. If you were there to take me to school and pick me up that morning, I would have been protected from those boys. For a long time, I started to hate you as a kid because I didn't understand why you were no longer coming home at night", Dominece said as she fought to hold back her tears.

I got up and sat beside her to embrace her. I needed to let her know that those days are behind us and that those hard times will never repeat themselves as long as I am alive.

"It's all right. I'm here now. Everything is going to be fine." I said to her.

"So Daddy, what are you planning on doing for work? You know the economy is in its worst shape in 30 years they say. People are being laid off every day." Tameika said to me.

"To answer your question, until I get my book published and make some money, my plans are to apply for General Relief (GR). It's all good, but as bad as it may sound, at least it's better being on welfare than being locked up," I responded.

"Amen to that," Tameika said.

"Mommy really never talked about your case, which left me and Jonice in the blind for all these years," Dominece said. "This may sound silly, but did you miss me, Jonice, and my other sisters?"

"Of course I did. I have a question for you, Dominece. Do you still love me the same, now that I have gone to prison, since I was not there for you, or are you ashamed of me?" I asked.

"I do still love you. That is something I could never stop doing as long as I'm alive. It's going to take some time before I can fully trust you as my father. When you trust someone and know that he or she has your back regardless, then they up and leave, just vanish out of your life that is a large pill to swallow. Jonice and I waited for three hours for you to pick us up. I even thought that maybe you got tied up with one of your business meetings and that at any minute you would be pulling up in your white Escalade, playing your oldies. That minute never came." Dominece said as she stared to tear up.

"Once again, I'm sorry. Daddy didn't plan to go to prison that morning. I was only supposed to make a court appearance, but the judge decided that he would revoke my Bond and had me placed into custody. There was nothing that Daddy could do, and I apologize for that," I said.

"Well," Tameika said, "I have a question that you may not want to answer, but I need to ask it anyway. I just want to know, why did you ask my Mom to have an abortion when she told you she was pregnant?"

"I didn't ask. I only suggested it because Dominece was barely a year old. Her mom had just moved in with me and I really wanted to make it work with her, but when your mother told me that she was pregnant, it took me for a spin. I didn't expect to have another baby especially back to back. Plus your mother and I weren't together; we had been broken up for two years," I answered.

"So I wasn't planned?" Tameika asked.

"No."

"Was I a mistake?" Tameika asked.

"No."

"Thank you. I needed to know that for myself. I heard so many rumors but I never heard it straight from the horse's mouth. Now I can put this behind me and bring closure to this chapter in my life," Tameika said.

"Tameika, did you get the letter I sent you?" I asked.

"What letter? I never got a letter from you, Daddy," Tameika answered.

"I sent you and Dominece a letter right after I received the Father's Day cards you all sent me last year. Did you get your letter, Dominece?" I asked Dominece.

"I got mine, in fact, I have it with me. I keep it with me to remind me that I have a Dad that loves me," Dominece answered as she reaches inside of her purse to find the letter I had written to her and her sister Tameika.

Dominece looked in her purse, "Here it is right here, Dad. I have it folded in my wallet."

"Let Tameika read the part that I wrote to her," I said to Dominece as I reached for the letter, and passed it to Tameika.

Tameika got emotional, "You wrote a letter to me, Daddy, how sweet. My mom told me that you were nice to her when you were seeing each other."

Tameika took a moment and read the letter.

"This is so sweet, Daddy. You are going to make me cry. Thank you. This is the first time anyone ever has written me something this sweet. Wow," Tameika said as she reached over and hugged me.

I stated to them, "The both of you and your sisters made me want to become a better father. When a daughter is born into this world, I feel every father has a responsibility to raise their daughters with tender loving care. We should give them guidance and teach them how to become Godly women so that one day, they will be able to make a positive impact in society. These days most fathers, including myself, do not fully understand the importance of the role of fatherhood, especially when it concerns daughters. Our duty is to protect you so you girls can later protect yourselves. I just hope someday my daughter's can find it in your hearts to forgive me for my absence and for neglecting my responsibility as your Daddy. I also pray that it's at the deepest level of forgiveness."

"Deepest level of forgiveness, I remember you explained that there were seven levels of love but you never said anything about levels for forgiveness," Dominece responded.

"Yes, There are seven levels of love and four levels of forgiveness," I replied.

Tameika got up to close the door while speaking at the same time, "Dominece told me about the love levels that you explained to her, but now you're saying there are levels for forgiveness? This I got to hear, but first let me close the door, because the music is so loud I can hardly hear what you're saying, Daddy."

"Ok, I said to both girls after Tameika returned to her sofa. The first level of forgiveness is when someone asks to be forgiven and you forgive them with some reluctance because you may be confusing the act of forgiveness with condoning their action."

I went on to explain the three remaining levels of forgiveness. The second level of forgiveness is when you don't have a need to let the other person know that you've forgiven them.

The third level of forgiveness is, you forgive someone but you never forget what he or she said or did to you.

The forth level of forgiveness is, when you forgive and forget. More often than not you have to spend some time grieving before you can open your heart to be able to forgive and forget. Can it be achieved? Absolutely, but it's easier said than done. Not too many people have the skills or the tools to release the hurt and pain they feel. Sometimes we need to take a real hard look at ourselves. Sometimes we contribute to the hurt and pain that was inflicted on us, but yet we expect the other person to take full responsibility for the wrong doing to us. Forgiveness is also a process, but when you are able to reach level four.

"Peace and serenity will enter into your heart and life will become less stressful," I said.

"I know I can forgive and forget, Daddy. I don't know about Dominece," Tameika said.

Dominece says, "I never said I couldn't forgive and forget, I just said that it may take me some time."

"It's all good, baby, take your time; I'm not going anywhere. I'll be right here when you forget what I have done in the past."

Then Tameika says, "Don't take too long, Dominece. You see what just happened to Michael Jackson. He was the same age as Daddy."

Dominece stared at me for moment without saying a word. Tameika and I stared back at Dominece then Dominece spoke.

"You know I love you. Dad, and I have already forgiven you in my heart and my mind has already started the process of forgetting," Dominece said as she walked over toward me with open arms.

The two of us hugged.

"What time is it?" I asked as I looked around Tameika's apartment for a clock.

"It's 2:35. Why, Daddy?" Tameika asked.

"I need to get back to the half way house by 5:00," I answered.

Dominece shouted, "After doing all that time, you still gotta spend time in a half way house?"

"Yes, but it's only for a few months. Before I leave I have something else I want to say to the both of you."

Tameika and Dominece gathered their kids and everyone walked me to my car.

"Say goodbye to Pa-Pa," Tameika told her two children as she assisted the little one with his hand to wave good-bye.

"Say good-bye to your Grandpa. Wave good-bye," Dominece told her two sons as she also assisted the smallest one with his hand.

I reached over and kissed everyone before unlocking the driver's door. Tameika asked, "Daddy, when are you coming back?"

"I'll be back tomorrow." I answered.

"When are we going to have the power talk?" Tameika asked.

"What power talk?" I asked.

Dominece stated, "She is talking about the power of the V, Daddy. I told her about the talk that you and I had the other night when I went back over Grandma's."

"Okay, when I come by here tomorrow, Daddy will put you up on the "Birds and the V's" talk, but not until then."

Imagine a woman who celebrates every time her body goes through changes, and she is proud to be a woman. She honors her experiences, and shares her stories with other young women. Picture a woman that trusts and respects herself, who listens to her own needs, and desires, and meets them with expectations. Imagine a woman who has lived through her past, and has prepared for her future. Imagine a woman who authors her own life, and refuses to surrender except, to her true self and God? Imagine a woman carrying her wisdom as a shield, one who has decided in her early years to not use her precious time spending it with good for nothing men. Imagine a woman who values the woman that lives inside of her and she values those that taught her how to be a lady. The woman who sits in a circle of real experienced women, learning the truth about herself, imagine a woman that knows how to lead without being lead, a woman who stands up for all women. I imagine my daughters being that type of woman."

I answered, as I got into the car, pulled off and blew the horn.

The type of love that touches the soul of a man is something that can only be experienced by a father and his daughter(s). Today, I felt that power of love.

Even though I wrote the seven levels of love, there's nothing in the world that can compare to the feeling of love when you have a daughter or daughters staring at you in the your eyes, and then she says, "I forgive you, Dad, and I love you." Wow! That felt so good hearing those words come out of their mouths. Believe it or not, this is the type of love I want to experience from a woman. When she says those three words to me my heart melts like cold butter in a hot frying pan. In fact, this type of love from a female or man is the level that one can only feel in the presence of God.

To forgive a person and forget what they may have done to you is a gift. Not many people have the ability to forgive, and also forget what the person did as if nothing ever happened. To reach this level of forgiveness your spirit-man or spirit-woman has to almost be on the same level as God, because God is the true forgiver and forgetter. This is not to say that this level of forgiveness cannot be achieved. It takes a person that is willing to do both. In some cases, I believe that this level can only be achieved if a person is at a level five in their relationship or friendship where a bond is between those two people and they agree to forgive and forget everything. This is a clear representation that neither person wants to ever lose the other person, and they refuse to allow such little or big things to come between their love for one another and their friendship. Just a few months ago I experienced this level of forgiveness. I experienced what I felt was a wrongdoing when I needed that person's friendship, but I had to forgive them, put it behind me, and move on. They say if you don't forgive others then God in heaven will not forgive you for your tresspasses so, I had to make a choice. My choice was to forgive and forget so that whatever has been stored up for me to have as blessings, wouldn't be blocked by the hatred I may have had for someone that I considered a friend.

Remember, if anyone wrongs you and you want to be blessed, you must forgive that person and forgive them for what they have done. Do you remember what Jesus said while he was nailed to the cross before he took his last breath? He said; "Forgive them Father for they know not what they do." And if you recall the Lord's Prayer it says; ". . . And forgive us our debts; as we forgive our debtors." It's all about forgiving those that wrong you and letting go. Not being able to forgive and not letting go only holds you back. It's you that is allowing something that someone said about you or did to you that can cause you to live in anger, and the person who said it or did it is gone about their own business. Many times people say things out of anger. They say things to express to you what they are feeling at that particular moment. They may say hateful things to cause you pain. They might make an untrue statement about you because they were hurt by your actions. Let's learn how to forgive and forget. This will only make you a better person.

T   E

H   N

E D

A WOMAN'S FIRST LOVE

The first man that a woman usually falls in love with is her father. This type of love starts at an early age. Little girls often say when they get married they are going to marry someone just like their daddy. Daughter's and dads have a special bond, when a father spends time with his daughter(s) he is demonstrating love and affection for her. These are wonderful memories that she will come to treasure. When she grows into womanhood the qualities and other attributes including love and the affection that she feels for her father, are the same ones that she will be drawn to in a man.

Father's should spend quality time with their daughters and get to know them. Love your daughter(s) and teach them how to love and respect themselves first, then others.

Simple things matter like:

* Tell your daughter you love her often (by phone, email, text . . .)
* If she's been away hug her and tell her you missed her when she returns.
* Kiss her and tell her to have a good day when she leaves for school or work.

*   Make one day out of the week a, FATHER and DAUGHTER day.

*   Take walks with her, listen to her issues and concerns.

*   Create an open communication policy 24/7.

*   Remind her how beautiful she is.

*   She should feel as though you are her protector.

*   Watch a movie with her from time-to-time.

*   Help with her homework.

*   Teach her not to be a follower, and how to shape her own life's path.

*   Teach her independency.

*   Explain the difference between being a woman and a lady.

A LETTER FROM THE AUTHOR

After writing this novel I now realize what actually gives a woman's vagina power. Collectively, men have paid untold amounts of money, and they continue to pay out more each year just for the opportunity to spend time with the vagina. I now understand why some women assume that it's their vagina that holds the power over men and money.

For example, a woman that has a confident walk, signifies prestige and power. How a woman speaks is construed as power, and in some cases a woman's words can pierce a man's heart. Then there's the woman's body language, like her posture, gestures and facial expressions, for instance when she is sitting or standing erect shows signs of independence and power. A woman's mannerisms represent distinctive behavioral traits, which are found in a certain type of woman. A woman's eyes are the windows of her soul, and with her eyes, she can look at you with an intensity that can be magnetic. She also has the ability to make intellectual judgments without speaking. When this type of nonverbal communication is used on a man it implies that the woman has an interest, or she is using a form of seduction, which can play with and control a man's imagination. A strong woman motivates others and shows a certain amount of mental power. A woman that is raising her child or children alone should show strength, leadership, responsibility, and dedication, in order to assure that the child or children have a solid foundation. A woman who lives by moral standards who has integrity and refuses to compromise her self worth also demonstrates a source of ultimate power.

These are some of the things that contribute to the P.O.V. in this society.

Remember, every woman has a vagina, but not every woman that has a vagina knows the power it holds. A woman's vagina should never be used to identify who she is. A woman should think of herself as being more than just a "Man Pleaser." A woman's worth should be valued according to her attributes, and how she presents herself to others. In other words, the Vagina should ALWAYS be valued as "PRICELESS."

THE REAL POWER HAS BEEN EXPOSED

THERE ARE TWO TYPES OF FEMALES
WOMEN AND LADIES

A Woman: Defined in Webster's dictionary; a female human, opposite sex of a male; wife, girl friend or lover: When a female turns the age of eighteen she has reached the age of a woman. She doesn't have to do anything to become a woman because it's based on your age and not the way you look.

A woman can very well be a woman of the streets, where she sells her precious body to strangers. Younger girls might believe after they have given birth to a child this gives them the entitlement of "Womanhood," when in fact, it only makes them a female child with a child. Many times people will mistake a woman to be a lady or they will use the word lady when referring to a woman not knowing that there is a real difference between the two.

A Lady: A courteous, decorous, or genteel woman: *his wife or girl friend was a real lady, with such nice manners.* **A lady** is the equivalent of a lord, the counterpart of a gentleman.

A lady is one who wears respect as a shield, and demands respect. This type of woman doesn't hang out late in the night roaming the streets. She's also obedient to herself. A lady is kind, out spoken when needed, gentle, loyal, honest, and dresses like a person that never wants to be labeled as anything other than a lady. She also has class, something that can't be purchased. Becoming a lady and developing class is something that is instilled in the home at an early age, usually by mothers. Of course, a mother must be a lady with class herself, if not she will have no idea how to share this knowledge with her daughter or daughters.

Being a lady is something that every female should strive to become. There are many benefits in portraying the lady that you are when dating a real man. Some men don't practice opening the car door for a woman but when he is in the company of a lady she will insist that her door be opened for her, not with words but by her actions. A man that recognizes a lady usually doesn't sit around talking about sex on the first date nor does he attempt late night booty calls. A lady rarely gets angry and never gets mad. She's diplomatic, and she has or displays the ability to deal with people in a sensitive and effective way. A lady is tactful, sensitive, subtle, delicate, discreet, thoughtful careful, prudent politic, clever, and skillful.

Becoming a **LADY** is the ultimate achievement for any woman.

THE SIGNS

Here are just some of the definitions of the signs that a cheating man will do while he's either married or in a relationship.

Waving to get Attention: When a man see's a woman that he finds attractive he may wave to her hoping that he can invite her to join him where he's sitting or standing. Clearly he doesn't give a damn about you one way or another.

Last Name: When a man introduces you to someone else using your last name, it's usually a sign that the two of you are no more than business partners or associates.

First name: When a man introduces you by your first name to others it's a clear sign that the two of you know each other, but have not yet been intimate, and it doesn't appear that he has a real interest.

Friend:
When a man introduces you to his friends or family member as his friend it means you're friends. Maybe the two of you have been intimate a few times, but nothing serious. There has been no decision as far as establishing a real relationship, or it could mean that he's getting to know you and a decision has not been made. Remember there are different types of friendships.

My Girl:
When a man introduces you as his girl means, he likes you and wants to start a relationship with you. It also means he's making a claim.

My Woman:
This means, he cares about you and his feelings are starting to grow. My Woman also indicates that lots of intimacy has already taken place. This also means he has no problem acknowledging the relationship the two of you have.

My Lady:
This indicates that he not only cares about you, but he also loves and respects you for who you are, and he wants the world to know it.

My Special:

It means that the two of you have created a "Bond" so deep, where no other woman would ever be able to break what the two of you have built and established. When a man introduces you to his friends and family and he says; "Let me introduce you to my special," that is the equivalent of being his wife or wife to be.

The Look:

If a man looks you up and down, as if he is examining your behind and breast, when he first meets you. He has already undressed you in his mind, and all he wants is sex.

Loans:

If a man asks you to loan him money hours or even days after meeting you, it's a sign that he could be an undercover user.

Car Doors:

When a man refuses or continuously forgets to open the car door for you, he is a man without proper manners and he lacks gentlemen ethics, however, it doesn't mean he doesn't care about you. This is a clear representation of nothing, but a man.

Table Manners: When a man takes you out to dinner and places his "Elbows" on top of the table, it is either a sign that he doesn't have any table manners or he could be a bit lazy because one elbow is supposed to remain in his lap and the other is used to feed himself. His right or left elbow should always be lifted up from the table.

Sex Dialog: When there is only sex dialog between you and a man you just met and there are no plans for the future for a permanent relationship, love, support, marriage, kids and retirement. He's not the one, if you're hoping for love and a long-term commitment.

The Nick Name Game: If a man wants to give you a nick name like, the initial "B" short for Brenda or "C" short for Cynthia could be a cover-up while he is talking to you in front of another woman.

Not Waiting: When a man drops you off and he refuses to wait until you're at least safely in the house, is a clear sign of a man that does not care about you or your personal safety.

Toilet Seat Manners:
Not placing the toilet seat down after using the bathroom when a woman lives in the same home is a sign of being inconsiderate and lazy.

A Simple Thought:
If a man doesn't pick up the phone to call you to wish you a Happy Birthday, Happy Mother's Day, Happy New Year, or Happy Valentine's Day is a thoughtless man and a thoughtless man could also be a sign of selfishness.

Selfishness:
If a man falls asleep immediately after sex without being concerned about whether or not you were satisfied this is definitely a sign of a selfish man and he believes it's all about him and no one else.

I Love You Too:
If you're the only one that's using the three words, "I Love You" in the relationship, is a sign that he's not feeling you the way you're feeling him. Be careful of the "I Love You Too" game. Most people especially men will say I love you too AFTER women have already said it to us first. Most men will say the three words out of guilt or in some cases, just to make you feel good at that time. In

fact he's sending you mixed signals and messages, only to appease you.

Forgettable: If a man forgets everything that has to do with you he clearly has a lack of importance for you.

Silent Words: If a man refuses to talk about being in a relationship with you after three months of dating. You may not be the one, or he's not interested in giving up his time. He may believe you have no potential of offering anything more than sex, because you already have given yourself to him intimately.

Absent: These are some of the most important signs that every woman should be aware of. Why is he absent on holidays? Why is he absent when his cell phone rings after a certain time? Why have you not been invited to his home? Why isn't your picture in his cell phone or photo album?

Embracement: If a man pulls away when you attempt to hug him, or he barely hugs you back. This is a sign that he's not as happy to see you as you are to see him.

Foreplay: If your man skips foreplay every time the two of you are intimate. This is a sign that he has no patience when it comes to you. The average foreplay should be 20-30 minutes if not more. This form of intimacy is a clear indication that he does care about you and what the two of you have.

Ignored Phone Calls: When a man ignores your phone calls repeatedly it could mean this is a sign that he's irritated with you, and he probably wishes that he never gave you his number. Constantly calling is also a sign of a desperate woman searching for love because she is lonely.

Lack of Affection: If a man doesn't show any real affection toward you in public, it is usually a sign that he's not comfortable with public display, or he doesn't want to let other women know that may find him attractive. It could also blow his chance of getting to know someone else that he finds attractive.

Lack of Attention: When your man or the man you're with isn't showing you attention. This is a sign that the man you're dating isn't really feeling you the way you want him to.

Signs of A Controller:

Here are some of the signs of a controlling man; Giving you specific times to meet him. Showing up at your job or stopping by your home at all hours without notification. Get's upset when you tell him "NO" that he can't see you. He is calling you consistently when you are visiting friends, or family, telling you to come where he is. He needs to know why you did not answer your phone. Demands you spent time with him. He tells you that he does not want to share you even with your children, friends, family or parents. Tells you why you should not be hanging out with any of your friends, by finding faults with them. Tries to isolate you from family and friends. A controller talks to your friends behind your back acting like he is interested in becoming their friend, but really trying to find out anything about you. Finds your weakness, and then uses them against you. They will use your past against you, to down grade you; to tear you down so you begin to have low self-esteem. He wants to control your finances. Controllers threaten to do bodily harm to you or your kids, if you try to leave him. He raises his voice at you in a calm conversation. Displays anger when someone looks at you if you look back or even speak to someone that spoke first. Wants you to fear him. Controllers are very secretive with their own life, but wants' to know everything about yours. He does not trust you, and always suspects that you are cheating and he will check the mileage on your car daily.

Signs of a Cheater:

Cheaters have many signs here are just a few of them. A cheater will lie about where and how much time they spent at a location. A cheater always checks his emails and messages; they never let their cell phone out of their site. Stops answering his cell phone when you're in his presence he talks in code. Never says the caller's name while he's talking. He never uses the Internet when you're around. His usual patterns and attitude changes, he starts arguments as an excuse to leave the house, or he stays out and doesn't come home until the next morning. He finds excuses not to attend family gatherings, functions and vacations. The number of times the two of you are intimate will decrease or he will not be in the mood. The amount of sperm he releases is minimal. He is always busy at work or with his boys. His touch will feel different and the sex lasts no more than fifteen minutes if you're lucky. Some say that the compliments decrease, but I feel differently, I believe he will overly compliment you, and send gifts like jewelry, and beautiful flowers, shopping sprees and other elaborate gifts. A man with a conscious will give you these type gifts because of guilt. If he rarely dresses up and suddenly he starts to dress up more often, this can be one of the signs too. If he's over weight and he's cheating with someone he really likes, question his weight loss, it could be for reasons other than health.

ASK JOHN, FIRST

QUESTION: Is it okay to have sex on the first date?

ANSWER: It depends on what you're looking for. If you're looking for a soul mate or a serious relationship, the answer is no. It could give a bad impression of you and he may think you are promiscuous, and think twice about being serious with you. Sex is supposed to be sacred, not given away in exchange for money, clothes, dinner or a happy meal.

QUESTION: Should I tell a man that I just started seeing how many sex partners I had in my lifetime?

ANSWER: Of course not, he will pre-judge you before the two of you leave one another's presence or before the two of you hang up the phone. Now, if your first date happens to turn into numerous dates, and it seems as though the two of you are becoming closer, consider answering his original question when the two of you first met, but not before he's told you how many sex partners he's had in his lifetime. Also, consider your age. If you're only 20 years old and you had 20 sex partners, you may want to keep that secret to yourself.

QUESTION: Is it okay to have un-protected sex because my boyfriend said it feels better to him when he's not wearing a condom?

ANSWER: Absolutely not unless he's your husband or your husband to be, even then, make sure your have papers on him, HIV/AIDS and STD papers.

QUESTION: How do I find Mr. Right, and not Mr. Right Now?

ANSWER: Know what it is you want from a Mr. Right, and I would not recommend looking in nightclubs and strip bars. My advice is; if his "Good" out weights his "Bad" and you can tolerate his "Bad" he could be Mr. Right but never accept mental or physical abuse.

QUESTION: Should I use my vagina as a form of punishment?

ANSWER: If you're married, absolutely not. If you're not married, it becomes your choice. Just remember the V isn't a toy, and it shouldn't be waved in some man's face to get him to do what it is that you want done. Games are for kids, not adults.

QUESTION: Is it okay for a woman to be alone?

ANSWER: Yes. A little alone time will allow a woman to gather her thoughts and make changes if they are needed in her personal life. You also need alone time to really get to know who you are.

QUESTION: Is there anything wrong with dating more than one man at the same time?

ANSWER: No, unless you're seeking a serious relationship. It makes it difficult to get to know a man when you're dating multiple men. But I believe in equal opportunity, what's good for a man should be good for a woman; of course society will judge you. Dating is to get to know someone without being sexual. Would an employer hire the first person that is interviewed? The answer is no. Give yourself choices.

QUESTION: Should I ever remain in an abusive relationship?

ANSWER: Hell no and that includes physical, mental or verbal abuse. I'm sure that some of you will feel the need to remain in an abusive relationship because of love. Read this carefully, love can be replaced; you can't, would a real man beat his mother? Never remain in that type of relationship.

QUESTION: Is it okay to fall in love with a man outside of your race?

ANSWER: Yes. True love is "Color Blind." Only prejudice love judges. Imagine if the entire world were blind. Would color matter? No. Of course be aware that some religions oppose dating someone outside of their race.

QUESTION: Is it wrong for a woman to ask a man for money when she barely knows him?

ANSWER: I see nothing wrong with asking however, what do you think he will say? Not knowing someone and asking for financial assistance could run a man off unless he has it like that and doesn't mind. Most men don't want the woman he is fond of to be a liability. He usually wants her as an asset to him. Today it's $10.00 for gas, tomorrow the Mortgage.

QUESTION: I am the mother should I be the first to tell my daughters about sex?

ANSWER: Yes. You have two choices. Either you talk with them, or they find out about sex in the streets and from their peers. The mistakes you made as a woman should be a lesson for your daughters.

QUESTION: If my man tells me he loves me after two months, should I believe him?

ANSWER: Do you believe true love can be established in two months? Did you feel love within two months? If you answered yes, then it's love. I'm old school. I still believe love at first sight, believe it or not, silly me. For all those that don't know when love comes, love is like an earthquake. You never know when it comes, it just comes.

QUESTION: How will I know if I have the V power?

ANSWER: Only you would know that answer.

o   Should I date someone online?

Ask John First

o   Should I date a co-worker?

Ask John First

o   Should I date a man that has a girl friend?

Ask John First

o   Should you tell your best friend that her husband is cheating?

Ask John First

o   Should I divorce my husband because I no longer love him?

Ask John First

o   Should I date a married man?

Ask John First

If you have questions regarding your relationship or concerns about a relationship decision, or if you need clarification or answers.

Visit, **Ask John First,** at

kistonebooks.com

TWELVE WAYS TO MAKE LOVE
TO A MAN'S MIND

Many have said: "The way to a man's heart is through his stomach." However, I believe the way to a man's heart, is through his mind. Make love to a man's mind and his heart will follow.

One: Recognize all of his good qualities and tell him all the things you like about him. Offering a compliment to a man can build up his ego and increase his confident.

Two: Never mention his flaws, or what you don't like about him when trying to get to know him.

Three: Find out what it is that he wants to accomplish in life and support him one-hundred percent. Remember, a man with a goal and purpose in life needs to know he's being supported.

Four: Never discuss sexual intercourse during the first few weeks and keep him from discussing it when the two of you are engaged in conversations. Making love to his mind is what is important and mental stimulation has more to offer during this stage of the possible relationship.

Five: Ask him his three favorite foods he loves and prepare those dishes for him at some point. A home cooked meal will remind him of his mother's cooking, where there was plenty of love.

Six: If a man has only been divorced for less than three years and he has not healed from the divorce. Give him time. Never discuss the divorce unless he brings it up. When he says negative things about his ex-wife you counter him by saying something positive.

Seven: A man with a broken heart needs to feel and believe in his heart and mind that you're the one for him and that he can trust you with his heart, which is why making love to his mind, is more important than making love to his body.

Eight: Promise him everything he needs, wants and desires, but over a period of time. Nothing should be given to anyone overnight. Stay away from dates and times. A man will hold you to it and can begin to dislike you if the promises you make to him are broken.

Nine: One day just out of the blue, ask him his shoes sizes, shirt sizes, pants sizes, coat size including his favorite colors, and the size of his underwear. This is a clear sign of a giver, not a user or some gold digger.

Ten: Be willing to go out of your way for him, make him feel first and important in your life. A man needs to feel special and connected believe it or not. When the two of you begin to discuss sexual acts, be clear to share with him the things you will and will not do. If there's a line you refuse to cross, let that be known to him up front. For those that don't have a problem crossing that line when it comes to sex. This will also increase his confidence in you, this is important, that he believes that his woman should cross those lines.

Eleven: When getting together for the first time for lunch or dinner, pick up the tab. This alone would gain you lots of brownie points. He's not expecting for you to buy him lunch or dinner. Un-expected acts are part of making love to his mind. This nice act on your part doesn't need to be repeated after the first time. A sense of independence can be very attractive to a man that's seeking love. No one wants to feel as though he or she is being used.

Twelve: Text or call him for the next five days; Once in the morning and once before going to bed. Ask him how his day at work was. Let him know that he's really important to you and that he is on your mind. Ask him what it is that he wants from a woman before he asks you what it is that you want from a man. Beating the man to the punch gives you the upper hand, and it allows you to remain in power. Making love to a man's mind is like discovering virgin territory.

TEN VITAL MISTAKES WOMEN
MAKE WHILE DATING

Here are a list of things that a woman should never do when starting to date someone new.

1. Never go into a new relationship with a broken heart, expecting the new man to help you heal your heart. This is something that you need to do before you start to date. It isn't healthy nor is it good for another man to become your personal psychiatrist. Repair what has been broken first, remember, a broken heart takes time to heal sometimes it can take years.

2. Never talk about an Ex-boyfriend, man or husband when dating someone new. A new man never wants to hear about a woman's ex. It means nothing to him, however, some men may ask you what happened in your previous relationship causing the two of you to break-up, but after you answer him. Bury that conversation and move forward. Only two things can happen, one, if you talk about your ex all the time when engaged in a conversation with the new guy, it would cause him to think that you still have feelings for your ex, and if you talk about how bad your

ex treated you, he will draw his own conclusion that maybe you have not healed from the break-up and your heart still suffers from pain.

3. Never hold a conversation with someone you have a real interest in while you are yelling at your children, trying you get them to do things like pick up their clothes off the floor or turn the television down. This can become very annoying to him. It can also give him a reason to think that you don't have control over your children. He may even think that you lack disciplinary skills when it comes to raising your children.

4. Never take your anger out on someone you just met because you're still angry at your Ex. Sometimes another man could inadvertently say or even do something that may remind you of your Ex. Every man should be treated as a separate entity.

5. Never change from the person you are because your ex treated you like crap. In most cases it isn't you to blame for the relationship when two people break up. Stop picking the same type of man and expecting a different result. Be open to someone new and different.

6. Never expect for the new man to live up to a HIGHER standard in order to make up for the way your ex did or did not treat you. Expecting more than what you feel you deserve isn't going to make you that much more attractive in fact, it could blow your chance of ever developing anything special or worthwhile with that potential someone.

7. Never tell a man you're looking for a husband or a soul mate on the first date. As we all know, the majority of men are afraid of the word

"Commitment," even a temporary commitment. A lifetime commitment could make him delete your cell number before saying good-bye. Did I mention it makes you sound desperate?

8. Never ask a man for money in the beginning of a relationship and DO NOT introduce your children to your new date as their; "Baby Daddy." This could make him vanish, fast and if he leaves anything at your home. He might count it as a loss.

9. Never have sex on the first date. If you're looking for love.

10. Never "Text" more than three times and never place a single phone call while on a first date, unless it's important and necessary. To text back and forth while engaging in a conversation or eating is rude and disrespectful, Your first may be your last date.

Meaning of the, V - Pendant

The type of woman who
wears this pendant is proud of her
shape, size, curves and color.
She is confident in the woman she has
become.

She does not minimize her beauty
or intellect. She is free from any
restrictions. She cares about
female causes greater then her own.
She is the reflection of possibilities.

While many women wear jewelry
as a fashion statement,
the V-Pendant is to be worn as
a statement of self-validation.

Become a Woman of Validation!
Order Your V-Pendant Today!

povdesigns.com